Oldest Daughters

What to know if you are one or have ever been bossed around by one

Patricia Schudy

Foreword by Kristin S. Russell, Ph.D.

Rudzik Press
Boulder, Colorado

rudzikpress@icloud.com

ISBN 978-0-9983865-0-8
ISBN 978-0-9983865-1-5 (ebk)

Library of Congress Control Number: 2017901689

Cover design by Ann Marie Greenberg

Rudzik Press
Boulder, Colorado

First Edition
Printed in the United States of America

To Rob,
who always encouraged me to be me

...there's another kind of hole,
and that is the wound that divides family.
Cutting for Stone, Abraham Verghese

Table of Contents

Introduction

I am the first-born child and oldest daughter in my family. I was followed over the next nineteen years by three sisters and one brother.

These facts played a determining role in what I would spend the past decade doing. It started innocently enough.

Over breakfast at a favorite neighborhood deli a longtime friend and I made a couple of unexpected discoveries about each other. We are both the oldest child in our families. That also meant each of us is the oldest daughter. We began to talk about why that was important.

Like coffee from the pot of our distracted waitress, stories about our first-child/ oldest-daughter experiences poured out and spilled over for the next two hours. We identified with each other's stories and sometimes commiserated so totally that we laughingly considered forming an ODA—an Oldest Daughters Anonymous.

That never happened.

However, in thinking back over our conversation, I came to a surprising realization. Many of the stories Barbara and I shared weren't about what we had experienced growing up. Rather, they revealed what was going on now with our siblings or spouses. That link between our family-of-origin position and our adult family relationships intrigued me. It set me on a mission to find out how other adult lives are affected by the oldest-daughter dynamic.

I began mentioning to friends and colleagues the possibility of writing a book about this topic. Responses burst forth immediately and almost always began with, "I can tell you ALL about ..." Everybody it seemed had a story about an oldest daughter, told with a range of emotions from admiration—and often humor—to exasperation. The one consistent was the main character. The oldest daughter who might even be the only daughter among siblings. And always, the anecdotes were about some interaction with the family.

In an attempt to understand why such surprisingly strong reactions, I talked to family therapists, checked out memoirs of oldest daughters and perused publications on birth order. The published research was skimpy. What I found generally referred to oldest children regardless of gender. I discovered that much of the data gathered from medical and sociological research has been based on males. But what about oldest *daughters*?

(Full disclosure alert—My interest was more than academic. I wanted to know more about oldest daughters for myself, as well.)

Next, I created an online survey to gather opinions from random first-born daughters who were not only children, siblings and spouses. This survey was designed to provide clues to important family relationships. It was never intended to be an academic study or to be described as demographically valid. I am pleased that several hundred responses came from individuals of every ethnicity and age group from eighteen to eighty. Information about the survey spread through word of mouth to some surprising places.

Most of those who participated had been born in the U.S. Others hailed from as far away as Great Britain, the Republic of Georgia, the Philippines, Cuba, the West Indies and New Zealand. Those from the United States represent this country's diverse ethnicities: Caucasian, Hispanic, African-American, Asian-American, Native-American and melting pot.

I deliberately kept the survey open over the several years it took to complete this book. Doing so allowed me to see which, if any, responses trended differently over time.

More individuals than could be accommodated offered, through a question on the survey, to share their personal experiences in follow-up phone interviews. I asked women I spoke with what it is like to have been the first-born daughters in a family, whether as oldest child or not. And I asked other women and men what it was like to have lived with an oldest daughter as either a sibling or a spouse.

One person commented, "Pat, you must be an oldest daughter to want to write this book!" Another came with a different perspective: "I can't believe I'm the only one who wants to know how to survive an oldest daughter." Repeatedly I heard both pride and pain when childhood expectations and/or responsibilities would lap over into adulthood.

Stories and comments are at the heart of each chapter in this book. They tell of struggles and successes, of life experiences and lessons learned, and reveal facets of family relationships often not readily evident. They include the person's age at the time of interview and a first name. If the "name" appears in quotes, it reflects the person's desire to protect personal or family identity. I've included background information important to the story. Occasionally I've provided an update from a follow-up interview.

Each of the book's chapters focuses on a specific aspect of life as or with an oldest daughter. Comments in "Other Voices" in Appendix I at the back of the book are taken from additional interviews. Attitudes and feelings captured in the survey data appear in the "Survey Snapshots" in Appendix II.

In some respects, this book is also a story of my own life. In each chapter's introductory comments, I share relative details about the impact being the oldest daughter has had on my life and on those closest to me.

It became clear as I conducted the interviews that often a need was expressed—even a yearning—to strengthen or mend relationships. What, if anything, could an oldest daughter, a spouse or a sibling *do*, other than talk about, vent, commiserate, or encourage through shared experiences?

For several months I discussed this question with Dr. Kristin Russell, a clinical psychologist who specializes in women's issues. It was easy to get her ear and opinions. She is my oldest daughter. I eventually asked her to add a professional perspective to each chapter's topic. Her bylined comments are found in "Professional Insight" at the end of each chapter along with her suggestions for individual reflection or family discussions.

In writing this book, my belief has been strengthened that *birth order is a fact; it does not have to be a fate.* Changing the mindset of "the way things have always been" to seeing "what's possible" became one of my primary goals. I was determined to be true to the intentions of those who shared their experiences with me in hopes of raising awareness and increasing understanding. I remain convinced that the position of oldest daughter affects a woman's life and relationships like no other position in the family. From childhood through adulthood.

When all is said and told, *Oldest Daughters: What to know if you are one or have ever been bossed around by one* is about relationships. About the way we connect with—and what we choose to expect from—each other.

It is my hope that as you read, you'll find yourself becoming more aware of the way you, your siblings and/or spouse function in connections with each other. That you'll consider possible ways to strengthen family bonds. Above all, I hope you will discover additional potential for joy in your relationships and in your own life.

Patricia Schudy
January, 2017

Foreword

My interest in the subject of oldest daughters is not a result of my birth-order position, though I am the oldest daughter in my family of origin. Rather, my interest as a psychologist specializing in women's issues is in helping oldest daughters and their families understand how developed roles may influence their relationships and their lives as adults.

Throughout my ten years of clinical practice, I have seen similarities in the experiences and subsequent feelings of some oldest daughters and their families.

I believe it is important to recognize that having the oldest children in a family assume responsibilities that younger children are not yet capable of doing is a reasonable and often necessary part of successful family functioning. It is also important for parents to encourage their younger children as they become older and more capable to share those responsibilities. However, that may not happen if parents are overwhelmed or if they believe the oldest children should have ongoing responsibilities for adult tasks.

Because females, more than males, have evolved to be responsible for children, the first-born female is often the one expected to step up to the plate, so to speak, and meet the needs of younger children. If roles developed in childhood continue into adulthood, they can impact—both positively and negatively—adult relationships.

To help the readers of this book further understand how their childhood roles affect both the choices they make as adults and the perceptions others have of them, I have provided comments in the "Professional Insight" section at the end of each of the following chapters. Following my comments are suggestions "For Reflection."

Both the questions and comments are intended to stimulate conversation about the specific issues raised in each chapter. They are not meant to place blame or judgments on parents. My experiences as an adult child in my family of origin, as a parent myself, and as a clinician have led me to believe that most of us are doing the best jobs we can, given our strengths, limitations and life demands.

It is my hope that this book helps oldest daughters become aware of and evaluate to what extent, if any, their ongoing role in the family affects their choices—and then to decide if they want to make changes for themselves. It may also be helpful for those close to oldest daughters to determine how these roles affect them, as well.

Kristin Russell, Ph.D.

January, 2017

There's nothing like being the first.
Common expression

Chapter 1.

Different

I am the first-born of five children in my family of origin, the "oldest daughter." The first time I realized that meant I was somehow different from others in my family, I was about eight years old.

My parents, two younger sisters and I had gone to my grandmother's Midwestern bungalow for Sunday afternoon dinner. I always looked forward to those meals—usually crispy, pan-fried chicken, heaps of buttery mashed potatoes puddled with creamy gravy and a cake Grandma had made from scratch.

On that particular day after we had eaten dinner but before we'd had dessert, my father took me into the kitchen. There on a linoleum countertop sat a small, white-frosted, chocolate cake. My father told me to cut it into six pieces. I did. My inexperienced hand created no two slices the same size. That's when the education of Patty as the oldest daughter began.

"Take this piece, it's the biggest, and give it to your grandmother," Daddy said. "Now, take this one, it's the next biggest, give it to your mother.... Now, take this one and give it..." until everyone in the next room had a piece. I remember thinking as he was going down the family line and fewer slices remained, "Hey, where do I come in?" I came in last and (you guessed it) got the remaining, smallest piece.

I sensed even at that young age that my father was trying to teach me an important lesson—not to grab the best for myself. I don't know if he also meant to leave me with the sense that others' needs and wants came before mine. But that's what slipped through to me. Recently I asked my younger siblings if our father had ever repeated this experience for their benefit. They can't remember any such lesson.

In his mind I was different. When my little sisters would do something displeasing, he would pontificate, "It starts at the top and goes down." How I hated when he said that. I would retort (in a thought that wisely never made the trip from mind to mouth) "Don't they have minds of their own?" No. I was to be the role model for my siblings. I had no choice or voice in this.

To be responsible, accountable, to learn as much as I could at school, to know the difference between right and wrong and act accordingly and ultimately be both a leader and nurturer in our family—these were the expectations my parents had for me during my growing-up years. I don't believe they ever changed these expectations.

My mother and father worked mightily to provide the circumstances that enabled me to become the first college graduate on either side of the family and the person I am today. It is only in hindsight that I've realized their unconditional love ultimately resulted in the opportunities and satisfactions I've enjoyed.

I never re-visited the cake-cutting incident with my father—the event that set the stage in my mind for what was to play out over the years.

In this chapter, you'll hear others' "aha" moments as they address the pivotal question: *Is there really something different about the role of an oldest daughter?*

Who's Going To Do It?

A first-born child, Tiffany became an oldest daughter at the tender age of two when her baby sister joined the family. She remembers herself as "a really skinny kid with long brown hair." Young Tiffany felt protective of her younger sibling, though at times she says she didn't really like her little sister very much. Nevertheless, Tiffany identified with her role in the family. She felt somehow special. That sense of status only grew stronger following a tragic event in her early childhood. Later, when her family circumstances changed again, the then-teenager's life became different in a way that threatened everything she had come to know and value about herself.

My mother died when I was six. For the next eight years my father raised my sister and me by himself. In a lot of ways I became like a surrogate mother. I would remind my sister to brush her teeth, help her get breakfast, scold her if she did something wrong. When afraid at night, she would sleep in my room. I felt very protective. Those things I took on because we lost our mother at such a young age.

There was no pressure for me to be in charge. I never remember my dad saying, "You're the oldest." I just took on the responsibility. It comes down to something very subtle. You kind of look around and say, "If I don't do it, no one's going to do it."

When I was fourteen, my dad remarried. I had mixed feelings. I was excited about having a new family and happy because my dad was happy. I was also scared. I sensed I had to be perfect. That was me putting pressure on myself. I couldn't anticipate what it would mean to be in a blended family and to be, in age range, the middle child. One brother and one sister were older and I had two younger sisters the same age.

I felt the loss of my position as the oldest—that perfect-child position. It was the role I had played, being responsible, excelling at school. When we blended and I became a middle child, I resisted. A couple of years later I would identify myself as the lost child.

Let me tell you, I did not want to be lost. In an effort to be noticed, to get the kudos I used to get, I held a job and made good grades, but it wasn't ever enough. My parents had to dole out attention to five. I needed more than they could give me.

I didn't feel even a little bit protective toward my younger step-sister, but my protective feelings toward my birth sister intensified. On one hand I'd really get angry with her for borrowing my clothes and makeup and not returning them; but if other people got mad at her, I'd side with her. We were definite allies—us against the rest of the family.

My older step-sister probably tried to take on a little of the oldest sister role, bossing us around a bit, showing off her age in the really obnoxious way older sisters have. I'm sure I would have done it too.

As an oldest daughter, I couldn't understand why others couldn't see the things I saw that needed to be done. Like, "Hello, can't anybody else see that the dishwasher needs to be unloaded?" If it's common knowledge, then everybody should be able to see it, so either they're stupid or they're lazy. Now I know that if I'm going to be doing it all, why should they get a clue? They don't need to.

I didn't gracefully take on the role of middle child. I always wanted that oldest-child role. I think it's because you get a lot of trust, kudos, and recognition for being essentially a really great kid. Who wouldn't want that? It carries you a long way. Being the oldest daughter is part of who I am. I've carried it with me my whole life, even when I became the middle child after my father remarried. A lot of who we are is ingrained even by the time we're five years old.

It's not often we get to see ourselves from a point of view other than our own. However, Tiffany got to do just that. She got to be an oldest daughter and then a middle daughter observing someone else in the vaunted role.

What happened to her as a result of her changing roles, she says, was very subtle. "Only through time can you go back and analyze it."

At age thirty-seven, Tiffany acknowledges flat-out that the pressures to be perfect and achieve, often associated with first-born children, came from within her. They include a sentiment common to oldest daughters—that if they don't take charge and do what needs to be done, it won't get done. Judging from the number of times I've heard this refrain, apparently the "if you just wait long enough, someone else will do it" gene is one that most oldest daughters don't inherit.

Sibling CEO

The stretch of states in the middle of the U.S. map that drops from the Canadian border southward into parts of Texas and the Gulf Coast is known as Tornado Alley. If you grow up there, you learn early on that when the sirens wail you need to take cover immediately in a safe place. You know that the sudden appearance of a dark funnel-carrying cloud out of an otherwise sunny, blue sky and its relentless, menacing march overhead signal potential devastation.

Linda grew up in Tornado Alley. Before she was a full-blown teenager, she was the oldest sister to eight younger siblings. She knew a lot about storms, both the ones that create warnings on the radio and others that unexpectedly rip apart what was once considered a safe place. She intuitively knew when either occurred that she had to be the responsible big sister.

I was brought up in a home with my mother and father who didn't let us participate in things that would get us in trouble. They held me accountable for my actions. I was supposed to be a role model for my younger siblings who looked up to me as the big sister.

I remember one time especially that I felt good about being that person. My mother had gone from the house. I was a thin, very small thirteen-year-old, but I was old enough to be left with my younger siblings when my mom was at work. There was a tornado warning on the radio. The wind was blowing. We were all afraid, but I wasn't acting afraid. I knew I was the oldest and I had to get my sisters and brothers to safety. I got them all together and we went into a large closet. It seemed like a lifetime, but was probably no more than twenty minutes until I heard the wind subside. It hadn't been an actual tornado.

I was thirteen, too, when I knew I was a big sister for a different reason. That's when my dad deserted us. It was a hard time for me because there were nine of us children. It was a hurting time because he left us without food, water, necessities. I remember my siblings crying. It tore me apart.

Today, my sisters and brothers see me as the spiritual head of the family, partly because I am a pastor's wife and partly because I'm the oldest. But those two things don't guarantee that things will be easy.

Fifteen years ago one of my sisters lost a child. I remember starting to fall apart, but one of my other sisters said, "Linda, you're the oldest. You've got to pull yourself together and hold us up."

It was different than with the tornado experience. Then I felt like I was the big sister. This time I didn't feel like that. I didn't have any control over the situation. But within the hour I realized I had to become the big sister and do what I was supposed to do, to help make the arrangements. Everything worked out. My sister went through the grieving process the way she should have. I felt pretty important knowing I could help my sisters and brothers.

On another occasion one of my sisters wasn't taking care of her responsibilities as a young, single mother. She had left her infant girl with me. She just left. I was very upset that she had done that. I called the authorities. She was very upset with me. We had some words. It was definitely important to me that we got back on good terms. It was important to her, too. We both ended up crying. Definitely I was holding her accountable, letting her know she shouldn't have left her baby on me like that. She understood. It never happened again.

When I was a little girl I wanted to be a teacher. I liked playing rock school. Later, I chose to become a teacher. When I wrote my Ph.D. dissertation, I put on the acknowledgment page, "To my nieces and nephews, cousins and friends, Remember Rock School!"

Now I am a teacher by profession, a retired elementary school administrator. I am tutoring full-time while I finish my dissertation. I love to spend my time and talent with other people. I call myself "sensational at 60." I have taken care of myself since my youth. I'm a vegan vegetarian, avid runner and power walker. I have a close-knit family and am president of a family business.

I became president when my next younger sister suggested we all get together as a family annually. We made the decision to form a family business and have officers. We've got it on paper. We have a license, hold monthly meetings, operate various enterprises. I believe it was assumed I'd be the president because I was the oldest. (Laugh) Nobody argues with that.

Linda's "aha" moments—weathering the storms of her life, creating safe places for herself and others, learning to be the big sister—carried her over a lifetime and set her down in a position of lasting family leadership. They were, some might say, what provided the wind beneath her wings.

When we had all but finished the interview, I asked Linda if she had learned anything about herself from recalling and telling her story.

"Yes, it really made me think of my role and the responsibilities I've had throughout the years. It makes me feel that I'm favored in the family, empowered. I hadn't consciously used those words before. It opened up insights that have been hidden for years that surfaced today."

Do circumstances, including birth order, make, break or define the person? This story raises that question. No doubt her parents' early expectation that she would be the role model for her siblings created a higher standard for Linda.

But would that alone explain why Linda decided to accept the role of big sister with its unknown responsibilities in the "hurting times" she experienced as a young teenager? Or why she chose to continue to fill that role as an adult, even when things weren't easy for herself or her family? Or why her siblings continued to look up to her, going so far as electing her president of the family corporation?

Perhaps a plausible explanation may be found in the way she'd always filled the role of the oldest daughter and her siblings' responses to her. From the outset they experienced a difference in her. They experienced that they could trust and rely on her.

What an Oldest Daughter Does

Sally is a woman of many descriptions. She is a married mother of four adult children. The daughter of an elderly mother who lives nearby in a large Midwestern city. A sixty-three-year-old professional designer. The oldest of eight siblings, four brothers and four sisters.

Also a true daughter of the Emerald Isle, Sally can regale a listener with humorous tales. These include what it took to help keep her younger siblings organized when they were all growing up. But later on a very different challenge confronted her.

What do you do, how do you respond, when something you could never have imagined while growing up is suddenly a grown-up reality?

She was a year younger than I. She's been like my left leg. She's been there all of my life. I've been there all of hers. We weren't particularly close. We didn't even get along all the time.

I arrived at her home last year the day before she died. Her eyes were closed. I sat down in a chair and took her hand. There was a half-smile and an expression, like contentment, on her face. I think she knew I was coming, though she hadn't asked me to. I was glad I was there, and she was glad. I had been there two weeks earlier when the doctor told her there was nothing more that could be done. Her daughter had said to me then, "We need you. We need someone to put their arms around us when Mother dies." So I said, "I'm coming back."

I'm the only one from my family who went back at that time. I'm the only one who thought of going. Some of my other siblings had gone out a few weeks earlier. Others made the decision not to see her again because they wanted to remember her as she had been.

When I got back home from that last visit, my mother said, "I'm glad you went to represent the family."

Of course I would go. It's kind of like it was my place. That's what an oldest daughter is.

I don't think my siblings get how I feel about them. I doubt they've thought about it much. I'm proud of them, not like a parent would be, but because they are good people. They stand on their own two feet firmly. We all call on each other's expertise. Maybe some of them lean a little on me, but I don't resent that.

I never resented being the oldest. It's an honor. I don't know whether my personality is such that it fits well with me or whether my personality developed because of my position. But I'm very comfortable with it and happy to have the status of being the oldest. I don't wish I didn't have the responsibility. Accepting responsibility becomes a habit, and you develop confidence because you've done it for so long. It comes from being the oldest, from setting an example, accepting responsibility and gaining respect in return. It's a good feeling.

Sally leaves little doubt that in her opinion, the role of oldest daughter is indeed different, one to be played out over a family's lifetime. She did more than accept the responsibilities of her family position. She embraced them. She says she doesn't know if it's a result of her personality or the position itself.

However, there is a possible clue in what her elderly mother said following Sally's return from visiting her dying sister. Their mother was "glad" that her oldest daughter had done what she did. No sense of any generational or positional competition. Only appreciation.

Maybe it's not just the attitude of an oldest daughter, but the attitude toward an oldest daughter that determines what's different about this position in any given family.

Professional Insight

I don't deliberately track birth order in my practice, although I do obtain information about family history, including how many siblings there are and what the birth order is. I don't put any emphasis on birth order unless it is raised by my client or unless the information in some way affects therapy issues.

What I have found interesting is that birth order doesn't tend to come up unless a person is the oldest daughter, although women in general often view self-care as "selfish." Women in the oldest-daughter position often link the issue of not taking care of themselves as adults with having had to take care of others while growing up. For many, the obligation to be responsible and to put others' needs in front of their own has been developed, if not intentionally instilled in them.

Even when they reach adulthood, oldest daughters—often more so than clients in other birth-order positions—tend to continue to feel responsible for meeting their parents' and siblings' needs. This tends to be the case whether or not they are also the first-born children in the family.

So is the oldest-daughter position in a family realistically different from other positions in the family? It certainly can be.

But I think a more important question in a family situation is whether the position should continue to be different once all the siblings are adults. At this point, adults should be sharing responsibility and recognizing and valuing the skills each person has developed.

For Reflection:

- *Have you spent some time alone with yourself to figure out who YOU want to be?*
- *Were different expectations placed on you while you were growing up because you were an oldest daughter?*
- *Have you thought about how you want to respond to the expectations now?*

Kristin S. Russell, Ph.D.

I am fairly certain that given a Cape and a nice tiara, I could save the world

Leigh Standley, Curly Girl Design

Chapter 2.

Born to Lead

Only four short years after I realized that there was something different about my position in the family, I discovered there was also something different about me outside my family.

I was a freshman in a co-ed high school that elected homeroom leaders. Homeroom 402 chose me as a co-leader along with a super-nice guy as leader. What amazed me is that the elections were totally blind. No from-the-floor nominations, no speeches or poster campaigns. My peers simply cast their ballots and the two students who received the most votes were designated the leaders. I remember being totally surprised and asking my young self, Why would they elect me?

What is there that says “leader” about a person? I’ve continued to wonder about that over the years.

I recently heard leadership defined as "the willingness to go first." I chuckled because the trait of leadership has been most often associated with oldest children. However for an oldest child, going first is not so much a matter of willingness as of necessity and reality.

Nevertheless, researchers explain that first-borns benefit from a unique combination of opportunity, encouragement to try new things, and the responsibility to lead younger siblings. Most of this research has focused on male oldests.

Out of curiosity, I did a little search of my own. I found biographies of amazing women leaders. Across cultures and generations, in every field from the arts to sports. From the daughter of former slaves in the segregated South to the British Royal Family. From the first women on the U.S. Supreme Court to Nobel Prize winners. Even a partial list is too long to include here [1], but the women share one common characteristic—each is an oldest daughter.

Not that all oldest daughters are famous leaders or all famous leaders are first-borns. Hardly. For most of us, opportunities and accomplishments come in regular sizes on smaller playing fields. I continued to find myself in leadership roles as a college student, in my career, in my

[1] For detailed list, see Endnotes following Appendix II

community, and in what I write. Taking leadership roles has come naturally.

In this chapter, "Anna" has observed the same thing about herself and others. She says she can almost always spot an oldest daughter.

Player Coach

A coach on the sidelines with a playbook in hand is a common sight. Athletic from her youngest years, April would have been used to seeing her coaches carrying playbooks.

Spectators watching her probably weren't aware that the young competitor on the field had to develop her own playbook for her life and family. They couldn't have known the matter-of-course obstacles that left her intimidated. Or that the opponents she faced were in her own family. That her playing field was more often than not a courtroom.

Now age thirty-four, April has instant replay of most of the above details.

My father got custody of us shortly after my brother was born. I was five. After that we were in and out of court. There were times when, as the oldest child, I had to make decisions for all of us—me, my little sister who was two years younger, and my brother. Decisions like who we wanted to live with.

In one of my memories, I see myself in a courthouse with my little sister and brother. I'm standing up, and they're on each side of me. I'm the one who has no emotion. I'm the tower of strength for them. We're against a wall, standing next to the benches outside a courtroom because we couldn't go in. At this point, I've already talked to the judge or the lawyers.

My parents are on opposite sides, not talking to each other. I seem to be so strong, but I'm really not inside. I feel like I don't want to disappoint either one, and I feel like I've betrayed my mother, in particular.

I chose not to live with my mother because kids always look for comfort things. My mother never had enough food in the house. She always had the electricity cut off. My father always had enough food and never had the electricity cut off. So if I had to break my choice down to one word, it would be 'stability.'

I would choose to be with my father where my life was stable.

But then my mother would come and kidnap us, and that would ensure another court battle. We went to court thirty-three times.

When we went to court, I was the one who took the lead. My dad was not literate. I went to the law library and looked up custody law. I actually wrote a brief when I was fourteen years old and presented it to the court.

My father also expected me to be the mother figure. He would say, "You're the oldest and I rely on you to do what needs to be done." I paid the bills and cooked meals since the age of ten and made sure my sister and brother were dressed and ready for school.

I really didn't have a childhood of fun. I wanted to make sure I excelled at everything. I was always making sure my grades were A's. In sports, I always tried to be the best. I took everything seriously. Because of all that intensity, I was always in the survival mode. In all of my pictures, I never smiled. I was either very serious or very, very sensitive. People always asked me, "Why are you so angry?"

As an adult, I've asked my dad why he would always call on me to write something or do something he needs.

"Why don't you call my sister or brother?"

"Because you're always there. I can always count on you."

I've wanted to share the responsibility when it got to be too much, but I couldn't.

He wouldn't give them the chance.

My dad was a great man. He just went through a lot. I was proud of our family unit. It wasn't like, "This is horrible. Our life stinks." Instead there was a lot of love, and this just happened to be our lot in life. My dad, for what he had to endure and the challenges he had, did an awesome job and we all love him very much.

The last part of April's story says a lot about the expectations her father had of her, including his summary: "I can always count on you."

That person he could always count on, the former athlete who competed in a variety of sports from childhood through early adulthood is now an executive in a sports-related field. She attributes her career success less to her athletic achievements and more to her experiences as the oldest of the three children in her family. "There are certain things I've been programmed to be as an adult that relate to my position in my family and in my career. Apparently I have a leadership role."

April says she is proud of the love, appreciation, and acceptance of circumstances that exist in her family. It could also be said that April's attitude and leadership are cause for family pride.

Out Front

Jennifer, now fifty-two, is the third-born of the children in her family and the second baby girl. She was the first baby to be born healthy. The first-born child, a boy, lived only a few days. The second baby and first-born female entered the world with significant cognitive disabilities. At age eight with the mental capacity of a five-year-old, this technically oldest daughter would be placed in a full-time care facility. Respecting her older sister's birth-order position, Jennifer won't call herself "an oldest daughter." But practically speaking, she held that position.

One day her mother sent Jennifer, her seven-year-old older sister and two younger siblings out to play in the orchard at the side of their house. As the small troupe wound its way on a path through blooming bushes and burgeoning fruit trees, Jennifer kept them entertained by pointing out grapes, apples and whatever else she saw growing, Suddenly she realized that everyone—including her older sister—was following her lead.

She was six years old.

My first sense of leadership was at that moment. It was simply a feeling of responsibility. No emotion. Just acknowledgment, an awareness of who I was in that group. The one in front. I knew intuitively they were not capable of doing what I was doing, that I was the one person who could lead this small group through the orchard. That they couldn't do it, but I could. I had that role, not better or worse, just more capable.

I don't want to deny or disrespect my oldest sister's position as the oldest daughter, though I didn't really see her as an older sister. We played together, but I was the one who was "in charge" if anyone was.

I like being in charge, knowing that when things happen in my family, I'm the one they lean on. From my perspective, my siblings expected me to be the person to look after them, to do what my parents needed, to be the person my parents would ask first.

I expected myself to be first, to be the person who was more able, faster or better than anyone around me. Just because I was older, it was easy. If we went for a walk, I would be the one out in front, the first in line. If we played Monopoly, I expected myself to win.

By the time I was a teenager my parents were focusing on all the other kids, and I was left to make my own decisions. My parents were wrapped up in their own issues. I kind of fell into things, fended for myself. I resented that my parents didn't provide more guidance. But I felt good about my successes.

I was the first among the children who was able to succeed and live up to the expectations my parents dreamt of. Even now on my own, the one thing I value is the sense of being a pioneer. I enjoy exploring and doing new things.

I believe oldest daughters take on more than our fair share of responsibility. I have always felt responsible for my parents and for my siblings. That sense came from my position in the family, from being more capable than the younger children to do things around the house. It didn't come so much from learning about it from my parents or anyone else, but from being in the position in the family.

I see myself as the functional oldest. When I recently read a birth-order book, I saw how much I had in common with other oldest children. It was like finding my people.

I seek out the role of leader time and again, whatever I happen to be doing professionally in the corporate world or personally. Being a leader comes as naturally to me as breathing.

Jennifer doesn't recall her mother giving her any specific instructions the day she and her siblings went out to play in the orchard. So what explains how a six-year-old child somehow knows and feels capable of taking on the responsibility of leadership? Hers were tender shoulders. Yet something inside that young psyche accepted responsibility without crumbling and continued to carry it. Nearly half a century later what she felt in that orchard, she manifests today in corporate meetings.

When being a leader comes as naturally as breathing, can it be said definitively that the person was "born" a leader? Or did the circumstances develop it? The question of nature versus nurture once again eludes an either/or answer.

Against the Odds

The saying has it that what doesn't kill you makes you stronger.

Fifty-seven-year-old Karen was only fifteen months old when her parents were told that their oldest child had to have one of her kidneys removed. And that she had one chance in a thousand of surviving the operation.

She became the 1 out of the 1,000. She would go through life with only one kidney. For some that health-issue would have suggested going carefully, avoiding risks. Not so for Karen. Having only one kidney was just a circumstance in her life, like many other challenging ones.

Karen grew up with her younger brother and sister on a Midwestern dairy farm in mid-twentieth century America. It was a part of the culture and times when "the way things had always been done" meant that men took the lead in the family, on the farm, in business. Unlikely that those around her would take heed of a girl who, when full grown, would be only five feet tall.

If you were a betting person, you probably wouldn't have put money on her attaining prominent leadership positions in government and nonprofit organizations on local, state and national levels. That's what this woman from the heartland did. But the real test of her leadership came when she was called on to lead her family through ironic, deja-vu events.

Being the oldest definitely gave me a head start in doing what I wanted. I had very little fear of trying to do something I wanted to do. That just might have been born in me because, logically speaking, it shouldn't have been that way. If anything, it should have been my younger brother who was brought up to be the leader because on a farm it's the guys, the men who are in charge. In farm life, the focus was on men. Women were never in charge of anything.

For my dominating father to let me be, to let me flourish was surprising. But my personality emerged as the person in charge. I was never afraid to be me. When I was growing up, I was called the "Little General." The name stuck.

I grew up feeling responsible for my younger sister and brother, and the feeling stayed. There's no question in my mind that's because of my position as the oldest daughter. My sister knows that. Ironically, her life was also threatened with kidney disease.

She was experiencing kidney failure that was not recognized by the hospital. A friend who is a nurse told me I needed to get her out of there. So I became "pushy" and insisted that she be moved to a major medical facility. My friend's advice, my pushy-ness, and the move to a different hospital saved my sister's life and then led to a kidney transplant.

After my sister rejected that first transplant, her doctors told us there was nothing else they could do. I told my father who was there with me, "We're not going to accept that." We told the doctor, "This isn't the answer we want. We need a doctor who can make it happen. If it's not you, we'll find someone else." That doctor then did more tests, found a cadaver kidney, and my sister's had it for twenty-four years.

I'm also the person responsible for her lawsuit against the doctors whose non-treatment resulted in her initial kidney failure. I got her the lawyer and testified in trial. The result: a multi-million dollar award for her. Looking back, I didn't set out to challenge the status quo or to make a statement. It was just a matter of being myself.

Karen was an odds-beater from the beginning. She did not back away from what could easily have been daunting obstacles. During our interview, Karen chose not to tell anecdotes about the well-known people with whom she has rubbed shoulders in public life. Instead she talked about where her leadership began and ultimately became most meaningful. For this "Little General," home provided both the training ground and the proving ground.

Is there is a direct correlation between the early training one receives in the family and leadership? Or is it, as Karen believes, something that is just born in the person?

The Same Difference

Until "Anna" was fourteen, she says she didn't understand that her life was different from that of any neighbor down the street. Then as the adolescent tendency to compare oneself with others kicked in, she became aware that the way she lived was different. That her parents had trained her from the time she was a young child to be the junior mother for her brother who was five years younger. That her peers didn't feel the intense pressure of responsibility that she felt. Though she doesn't recall feeling resentful, she does know that she was determined to change her life as soon as she could.

When she went away to college at age seventeen, she was ready to leave her parents and the junior-mother role behind her and begin a new life. She wouldn't recognize then that what had set her apart from the neighbor down the street would stay with her and mark her for life.

The benefit I've had of being raised the oldest daughter is that I have been willing to step up and therefore I've tried new things. I challenged myself to change my career, to keep learning, to work on cutting-edge projects.

Even after I left home, moved across the country, lived with roommates, became involved in all sorts of things, I always just surfaced as an oldest daughter, as a leader. It's not like you can step out of it if you're in a different environment. It's in your training.

Right after college, I became a VISTA volunteer. That began my life in the area of service and in job creation as a method to alleviate poverty, in civil rights, the women's movement and the environmental movement.

The single thread that goes through my experiences, whether in the area of creating businesses or jobs or work for individuals, is that they were all cause oriented. Most recently, for six years—until I returned home to take on the responsibility of caring for my parents—I was vice-president of a non-profit organization focusing on economic development and the environment.

I've noticed I have more women friends who are oldest daughters than in other family positions. We often have the same kind of responsibility, and we rise in the work that we do either inside the home or outside.

There's a recognition of the role you continue to take—leadership—between women who are also oldest daughters. We recognize each other and we tend to understand each other well, often without having to define it. There are a lot of commonalities in ethics and values and goals. I think they/we became responsible to take care of things in the family, and that's the training ground for what we do in our work and personal lives.

I have had the greatest fun doing it. I created my own projects, got funded with millions of dollars of financial support and have been able to travel all over the world, working on projects. From working with bushmen in the Kalahari in very remote areas, to being at the Velvet Revolution in Czechoslovakia—I have truly had such wonderful opportunities and I've loved it.

As far as Anna is concerned, her course in life had its impetus in her childhood upbringing. She's also observed that, oddly enough, she has more women friends who are oldest daughters than in any other family position. And that these friends tend to be leaders.

I wondered if the same would hold true in my life. I was surprised to realize that from seventh grade through high school, college and after, socially and in business, the girls/women with whom I had the most in common, made the easiest and most lasting friendships—with a few notable exceptions—were oldest daughters. None of this was conscious. I never ran an ad, "Wanted: roommate/friend: must be an oldest daughter." It just happened.

I also created a personal check list of what these friends have done. No one has become "famous." But most are known in their own communities (and in a couple of cases even beyond) for having stepped up to take or fill a leadership position.

After sharing her story, Anna wondered aloud if "there is something that links oldest daughters beyond what I am aware of." I'd have to ask the same question.

Professional Insight

Nature v. nurture. The ongoing debate. Which is the stronger influence on who you become? The general consensus is both. Birth order, how we are parented, situational event—all influence which genetic traits become evident.

Leadership is a trait often associated with oldest children, regardless of gender. It's just common sense that since the first child is almost always the first to do everything, their younger siblings will follow them. Since first-borns are normally more advanced developmentally than younger siblings, more is often expected of them. That develops responsibility and may result in their taking a lead role to solve problems.

So for many oldest daughters who are oldest children, taking the lead, becoming a leader, is very natural and becomes one of their strengths. It is also human nature to step back if others are doing the necessary work. Consequently, there may not be the same impetus for younger children to develop leadership traits. But what may be seen as a blessing by them in childhood may also be a curse, or at least drawback, in later life.

Ideally, every child should have age-appropriate expectations and opportunities. Realistically, that is not always the case. So when they reach adulthood, most people continue without thinking to use whatever skills they developed as children.

It's important for every woman—regardless of birth order—to evaluate whether these skills are ones they want to continue to use and to realize they have the power to choose if, when and how to use them. For oldest daughters, that includes considering in which, if any, situations they wish to exercise leadership.

For Reflection:

- ☐ *Do I normally/naturally demonstrate leadership skills that others recognize? If so, how do I want to use them?*
- ☐ *Do I take leadership roles because it's expected of me or because I want to be in the lead?*
- ☐ *Are there situations or circumstances in which I no longer wish to take on a leadership role?*
- ☐ *What would be the consequences for me and others if I choose to change?*

Kristin S. Russell, Ph.D.

Labels are for cans, not for people
Anonymous

Chapter 3.

Brought Up to Boss

The opening episode of ABC's *Modern Family* in 2011 depicted the series' three interrelated families off to a dude ranch for a family vacation. It didn't take the ranch foreman five minutes to brand Claire—an oldest daughter/sister, spouse and mom—with the name "Bossy." It's a label she immediately resisted and one which became a burr under her saddle throughout the episode.

My personal "episode" occurred, not on a dude ranch, but in a nursing home. My mother had become a resident there years after a massive stroke resulted in the paralysis of the left side of her body.

As a regular visitor as well as having the durable power of attorney for her medical care, I had come to know well the facility's nursing staff. One day, headed for her room, I was abruptly stopped by the unit's charge nurse. "Your mother is refusing to take a shower," she began. Then she chuckled. "I have to tell you something she said when I told her, 'I'm going to call Pat.' She told me, 'Don't do that. She's too bossy.'"

I laughed, but my internal voice said, "What? My mother said that? My mother who guided my growing up with love and also trained me in family responsibility? Who encouraged and praised me my whole life? My role model? Said THAT?" To my knowledge, I'd never been called bossy by anyone in my life.

Down the hall to her room I went. I tapped on her door.

"Who's there?"

"The bossy one."

"I'm not taking a shower."

Smiling in rueful admiration of her still-present spunk, I went inside. She was lying down, eyes closed, mouth set in determination.

"So you think I'm bossy?"

"Sometimes..." Her voice had softened a little, become a little gentler.

"What would you suggest I do?"

"Stop being so bossy."

It was all I could do to keep from laughing out loud. Or maybe crying. I wasn't sure which.

ABC's sitcom and my own situation raise several questions. Does being called "bossy" bother most real-life oldest daughters? What about the word "controlling"? Fair descriptions that come with this position in the family or unfair stereotypes? What effect do such epithets have on an oldest daughter's self-image or on her siblings' ongoing perception of her? How much of the behavior of adult oldest daughters is about retaining the control enjoyed or required in childhood?

Two oldest daughters tell their stories and share their feelings about this topic in the next several pages. For them, "bossy" and "controlling" may not be "fightin' words, pardner," but they certainly can make a person skittish.

The Leading Lady

When twenty-four year old Sarah and her younger siblings were growing up, the family frequently watched *The Ten Commandments.* One scene in that movie classic directed by Cecil B. DeMille and starring Charlton Heston is especially familiar to them. Heston's Moses must choose a wife from among seven sisters. Their father Jethro encourages him to pick his first-born daughter, saying "She's the oldest. You'll learn the most from her."

It's not clear how DeMille came to characterize Zipporah that way because the Book of Exodus gives no personal information about her. Nevertheless, Sarah says, "Everybody in the family knows that quote. That would be true of me."

What made it true, and how being in that role continues to play out for Sarah and her younger siblings, is the stuff of which real life is made.

I have two younger siblings. My brother is a year younger than I, and my little sister is five years younger. Being the oldest daughter has made me a really strong and independent person because I had to blaze the path and figure things out on my own. If you don't have an older sibling at home and have their friends to watch, you have to do it yourself. By trial and error. I was expected to know the difference between right and wrong and to share that with my younger siblings.

I don't know if it's my personality or because I'm the oldest, but I've always wanted to be perfect and the best at everything. I really feel like I'd better be good at everything I do because the family is watching me. Part of me thinks that's because as the oldest, I wanted to be the leader for my brother and sister. There's also a little bit of sibling rivalry here. The pressure came from within myself—not wanting to get behind or let them get ahead of me.

I feel that oldest daughters have a double responsibility—to lead and to protect younger siblings, whether they're male or female. It's that nurturing, caring side that women have that men don't and that makes you feel more responsible about protecting your siblings. I've been really surprised at how quickly my claws can come out if I think a sibling's been taken advantage of.

Do I consider myself controlling? Yes! I try to control my relationships with my boyfriends and situations at work and in the family. I don't mind that aspect of my personality. I don't think my siblings would say I'm overbearingly controlling, but they'd say I'm controlling.

Even now when I go back home and my brother and sister are there, I see it in something as simple as going to church. I want to drive. I want them to leave when I'm ready. When I've finished talking after church, we're going to go. I think back to when we were all at home and I was the only one who was a driver. I guess I still like having that control.

I believe the oldest daughter in a family should continue to fill her role as the leader when she's an adult. My mom has a chronic illness. I definitely feel that it's my responsibility as the oldest child to do everything I can to make sure that we are doing everything possible for her, but I don't think my sister and brother are as worried about her as I am.

I'm pretty happy with the responsibility that's on me. I like to have control over things.

In the movie that Sarah and her family watched during her growing-up years, there is no indication that Jethro's daughters felt any competition with each other. But that was Hollywood. In the real-life version, adult Sarah feels a sense of rivalry with her younger siblings.

In what could be described as her personal portfolio, she claims credits for three roles. Zipporah-like, she performed as a mentor. As the chronological oldest in the family, she played trailblazer for her siblings. Then she got the coveted part as the solo driver during the teenage years when who has the car has the star power. Even years later, she admits she's reluctant to relinquish the control that came with it.

As her siblings also got older, Sarah has realized that her role as leading lady could be unexpectedly challenged by the accomplishments of her "understudies." No one, however, is competing with her for the caregiving of their mother. Perhaps that's why she now sees herself—as have so many Broadway and Hollywood stars—in a new position, the responsible Director.

The Unliked Word

We met fifty-four-year-old "Anna" in the previous chapter. As the storyteller of "The Same Difference," she credits the position of oldest daughter for developing the leadership that's led to her life of professional opportunities and rewards. In the following story, she flips the coin and addresses the position's negative stereotype and the double-edged conundrum it has created in her personal life. Even in print, it's possible to hear her frustration as she begins.

Am I a "controlling person"? I guess so. But I don't like that word, and I really don't like that terminology as a description of what I am or what we as oldest daughters are. Although if I asked my brother, I'd have to say he would probably say yes.

Because I was trained as a young child to be the junior mother of my brother, who is five years younger,

I don't think I really had a brother-sist with him until we were both away from h

Then when my father was dying a fe tension existed that could have actually parted us. So we made a pact that nothing was going to come between us as it has divided lots of families. We chose to deal with it upfront because we didn't want that to happen. We tread very carefully. We really do try to be clear with each other.

He's asking me now not to be controlling. It's hard because I do assume the responsibility. In the beginning I didn't realize he had any resentment about the way I was operating.

There was one intense, long, awful period when we had to make difficult decisions about our father's health and care taking. I took on the lead position in dealing with the attorneys because I'm the executrix, the one legally responsible. The stress for me was extreme. My brother became very angry about my controlling the situation—even though I had to take the responsibility. He did not like a decision I made and that I hadn't consulted him about before making it.

My brother does not like taking a back seat to my decisions, and so I have to step back often and give him time to think. We don't operate the same way, yet we have a lot of respect for the way we differ. We've had to be upfront about how that is and how that works. For instance, I didn't realize my brother needs more time to think about things, or if not, he feels he's having things crammed down his throat. We've both had to step back and visit those decisions, mostly in a loving way.

Now that I have become aware of the issues he has with how things should happen between us, I'm much more careful. That doesn't mean I've completely changed, but I have tried to communicate better instead of just assuming he's going to agree. It's very hard. It's one of the reasons why we made this pact. We don't want a rift to develop that would mean we'd never be close again. Both of us agreed to try to be as clear as we can with each other and not to assume that just because I think it's going to be fine one way, that he's going to agree.

In a lot of situations, even though I may be resentful, I never let my resentment be the knife that divides the relationship with my brother.

Ultimately what is most important to Anna is her relationship with her younger brother and only sibling. Fortunately it's important to both of them. But that doesn't mean she has shut down her feelings or the questions that continue to nag her. Why are there generally accepted, different responsibilities for a first-born female than for the first-born male? Why is the expectation to "take charge" perceived as "taking over"?

These questions can create a serrated edginess dividing resentment, resignation and resolution. Anna and her brother are taking the sometimes difficult steps to ensure clear-cut communications and the subsequent good relationship that is important to both.

Her stories in this and the preceding chapter point out the reality that few, if any, of us, lead a one-dimensional existence with only one factor influencing the quality of our lives.

Professional Insight

When an oldest daughter is told, "Dad and I are going out tonight, make sure everybody is in bed by 10..." Or if an oldest daughter is repeatedly put in a position of responsibility or authority with statements like, "Make sure your little brother doesn't go out in the street, or make sure your sister walks home with you after school."... And she tries to make sure everyone does those things, chances are she's not going to be very popular with her siblings.

If she doesn't make her siblings do those things, chances are Mom and Dad aren't going to be very happy with her.

Whichever choice she makes, someone could end up giving her grief.

Learning how to exercise authority without coming across as bossy is tough for kids. Learning to tolerate internal distress when others aren't okay with the choices being made can be tough for both oldest daughters and younger siblings.

If younger siblings choose to continue going to an oldest daughter for advice or approval, the oldest daughter may resent it if her advice is not followed. On the other hand, if the oldest daughter continues to try to influence or tell her siblings what to do, a younger sibling who chooses to continue acquiescing to an older sister is only reinforcing the older sister's role.

In adulthood, it's sometimes necessary to feel uncomfortable if you choose to meet your own needs instead of pleasing others. Change is hard.

If we are going to honor our own feelings, then we need to learn to express them and act in ways that align with who we want to be as adults, regardless of whether others are accepting of our choices.

This is easier said than done, as learning to tolerate distress is a skill that requires practice, just like learning a new language. If we didn't practice speaking new languages, it would never become easier and natural. Eventually, as we practice distress-tolerance, taking care of our own wants and needs versus complying with others' needs or wants in order to avoid conflict becomes easier.

For Reflection:

- *Do I communicate assertively with others or tend to be bossy, demanding?*
- *Do I "take control" of situations that are not mine to manage?*
- *How do I feel when others, especially younger siblings, make choices that I disagree with?*

- ☐ *Do I ask siblings, my spouse or a colleague if they want my opinion or do I try to force a change or express an unwanted opinion?*
- ☐ *How can I learn to suppress my opinions when others aren't asking for them or when they are unwelcome?*
- ☐ *Have I received feedback from others that I "tell" others what to do instead of asking or discussing with them?*
- ☐ *Would it be helpful to ask them to let me know when I am doing this so I can begin to change the way I communicate?*

Kristin S. Russell, Ph.D.

Who in the world am I? Oh, that's the great puzzle.
"The Pool of Tears," *Alice in Wonderland*, Lewis Carroll

Chapter 4.

Little Mothers

The youngest of my parents' five children was born when I was nineteen years old. Over most of her lifetime when we went anywhere together, people assumed we were mother and daughter. I would immediately clarify that "while I would be proud to be her mother, I am in fact her oldest sister." Admittedly there was a little age-related vanity lurking behind this statement.

She had been adamant about the distinction from the get-go. Not just with regard to me but also with her two other older sisters. As a young child she would stand—short blond pigtails hovering over her ears and hands defiantly on hips—and tell us one at a time or together that we weren't her mother. That role was already taken.

My then four-year-old sister was precociously wise. She intuitively knew there's a significant difference between sibling connections and a parent-child bond. However, circumstances can result in sometimes necessary muddling of the two as attested to in stories in other chapters.

In our family that happened just as this youngest sister of mine was practically all grown up and a freshman in college. In the spring of that year, while our parents were many hundreds of miles away on vacation, our mother had a massive stroke. It resulted in the entire left side of her body being paralyzed. The trauma necessitated immediate months of hospitalization and rehabilitation.

Early on during that time, my sister asked if I would go with her to a mother-daughter tea. Of course I said yes. Surrounded that day by other girls and their mothers, I thought of the legal phrase *in loco parentis* (in the place of a parent). That's what I felt like. A stand-in. A substitute. I had only to look into my precious youngest sister's eyes to recognize an ache that needed no translation.

I later learned from friends of my mother that for years she had referred to me as "Little Mother." This honorific sounded horrific to me. The intended title of honor was not one I would have chosen or ever wanted. I knew Mom had meant it as a compliment. That's what it had been in her generation. Perhaps she was remembering when we were co-conspirator Santa Clauses or early on when she would send my two little sisters in my care to the park across the street.

However, "Little Mother" was not my position with those two sisters when we were all in elementary and high school. I am four years older than my next sibling and five and a half years older than our next sister. Those are chronological age differences, but circumstantial factors separated us by several classroom years. By the time I was in high school, we had little in common. The only way one might say I acted as a little mother during those years is that apparently I described the facts of life to them as my mother had so lovingly told me years before.

It was not until I had graduated from college and they were in high school that we began the relationships we now have. Because I was the first one to have a career, a wedding, babies...I shared these experiences with them as someone who'd been there, done that, as the saying goes. I wanted to give them the benefit of my experiences, to be a protective advocate for them when I could. Doing so didn't make me feel in any way like their mother. I also wanted their opinions and advice.

My thirteen-years-younger brother, by the way, wanted no part of any of the above. Our experience was different. When he was a teenager and had gotten into a row with our father, he came and stayed with my husband and me until things cooled off. He wasn't looking for a little mother when he appeared on our doorstep. He wanted a sibling who understood the family dynamic.

If you were to ask him about that incident today, there is no doubt in my mind he would say he saw me as his trusted big sister. A trust I believe that links us, endures, and goes both ways. I treasure the mostly unexpected experiences I have with him these days, especially the times he somehow seems to know when I need a brother to lean on.

Being a sister to my siblings remains my personal position of choice.

This chapter's storytellers give an insider view of others' preferences and what can happen over time to an oldest daughter's self-perception as well as to her relationship with her siblings if she has unwittingly taken on or been assigned the role of a parent. They also share what is possible to enjoy in adult sibling relationships when childhood roles can be outgrown.

New Playbook

A "slightly buck-teethed, ten-year-old with curly hair like a French poodle and a bad case of acne."

That's how Pookie remembers herself when the life she had known and liked changed forever.

It was a warm day in May, a perfect day for hopscotch, jumping rope or simply hanging around with friends. This pre-teen and a cousin were playing outside the apartment house where she lived. But then her mother, just back from a doctor's appointment, called her to come inside. Uneasy, Pookie left her playmate on the sidewalk and walked reluctantly up the stairs.

I thought I was in trouble; but it wasn't the kind of trouble I thought.

Mom said, "You have a little sister on the way."

My first reaction was,"Dang, that means I'll have to share, be responsible!" My friends had always told me wherever they went, whatever they did, they always had to include younger siblings. As an only child, I had had freedom. I could do anything.

Three months later my mom came home with this little girl with a cone-shaped head. She had that new smell and was just so cute and little and quiet. I liked her until that evening when she wouldn't go to sleep and kept crying. Then I thought, 'This is it. I'm done."

After that it got worse because I didn't want to give her a chance. I didn't want to hold her. I wondered what my friends would think. I was worried about my reputation. Actually my new situation didn't even phase my friends.

I decided on her first birthday that I would finally accept her, though she wouldn't have known how I felt. I thought she was goofy. I could do anything to her and she'd just laugh.

Down the line, being an oldest sister even started to feel special and good.

I remember sitting on the floor at home with my little sister when I was fifteen and the magic light bulb went off. I realized my mom had actually given me more attention since my sister was born. It changed the way I thought. I decided I wanted to be a better big sister.

That feeling stayed until I was eighteen. At that time, my mom was a substitute teacher and was also going to school in the evenings, so my sister was often left in my care. I was in an adult situation. I fed her, bathed her, kept her safe, answered her questions, and was the disciplinarian. One evening I had told my friends I was going to do something with them. Instead I had to watch my little sister. I was hot under the collar! I figured out, "I don't want to do this anymore!"

So the morning of my high school graduation, I told my mom, "This is your child now." I felt free. I felt like I had done what I was supposed to do, to be a good role model, be a decent sister, teach her what I knew. I'd felt like a little mother. Now it was time to lead my own life.

By the time she shared her story, Pookie was twenty-eight years old and holding down a full-time job while completing her bachelor's degree. She reflected on what it had taken to get her to that point.

"I think if I hadn't become 'an oldest daughter,' I would have made different choices for myself. I might be lazy and spoiled. I probably wouldn't be working toward a career. I probably would have depended on my mother and let her provide for me. Instead, I feel pretty good now about being my own person. I still try to make sure I fulfill everything I can for family. I think this is the real me."

Pookie's story of herself as an oldest daughter is filled with refreshing candor. Because she doesn't sugarcoat her vivid memories, we are able to get inside the mind of a pre-teen, then an adolescent, and finally a young adult as she rides the emotional ups and downs from only child to older sister to little mother and finally back to herself.

Act II

You are eight years old. Your father has died. Your mother is a young widow. You have two little brothers. One is barely out of toddlerhood.

This is the difficult reality that Jen, now thirty-one years old, remembers. She used to think it set the stage for her childhood. However, she now believes another fact has played an even more significant role throughout her life.

Being both an oldest daughter and the oldest child defined my childhood in different ways. The oldest-child part was critical primarily because I was raised by a single mother. As the oldest kid, I was the one required to step up and help Mom.

My mom was herself an oldest daughter and oldest child. There were some expectations and beliefs intrinsic to her that because I was a daughter and a female, I would help her in certain ways—care for my brothers, make dinner, the sort of things I don't think an older son would have been expected to do. My next brother is only sixteen months younger than me. I don't think he ever had those kinds of duties when he was growing up. I was the one always helping in the kitchen, making sure my brothers ate dinner, picking them up from Scout meetings on my bike before I had a driver's license—traditionally mom or female roles.

I think I probably fit what people think of when they say, "oldest daughter"—the one who takes charge.

Looking back, (sigh) I think the most impactive result of having been both the oldest daughter and the oldest child has been playing the role of pseudo-mom in my brothers' lives. I filled in when my mom couldn't be there, which was a lot.

I don't think my brothers had expectations for me. I just existed. We all just learned how to take care of each other. If Mom wasn't around, if I didn't do those things, they'd have been disappointed in her—not me—because it was Mom who was supposed to be doing those things—not me—and they knew that.

My whole life had always been about being the responsible overachiever. That never changed. Always the expectation. It was incredibly overwhelming. I feel like my mom could have toned it down a bit, and I would still have accomplished as much as I have. God knows she didn't put these expectations on either one of my brothers.

She probably recognizes that, but we've never talked about it. If we did, I think she would say that I was her daughter. That's how things were when she was growing up, and that's how it was going to be.

If I had had the chance, I think I would have said to my mom, "Even though I didn't ask to be in this role, I'm trying my hardest to live up to the expectations. You of all people have lived this role. So maybe you could take the pressure off a bit. Because you should know how stifling it is."

One would think hearing Jen's story that her mother would have had fewer expectations of her oldest daughter, given her own identical birth-order position. However, other oldest daughters whose mothers were the youngest or middle child in their families of origin have expressed the opposite belief. They feel more was expected of them precisely because their mothers hadn't experienced being the first-born female in the family and so couldn't understand the pressures.

It seems that the problem, therefore, doesn't lie so much with the mother's own birth-order position, as with a failure to recognize what's reasonable or appropriate to expect from first-born daughters. As Jen states clearly, if briefly, her belief is that the expectations placed on her but not on her brothers were simply because she is female.

Some of Jen's most telling comments came toward the end of our interview when I asked what impact being the oldest daughter in her family has had on her adult life. She quoted a boyfriend who had recently told her, "I don't know if you've figured it out yet, but you take care of everybody." After repeating that, Jen said, "I'm on the fence because I don't want to take care of everybody. I want to be taken care of. But I think if I wasn't taking care of everybody, my self-evaluation as a person would decrease."

Old habits, as the saying goes, die hard. Evidence two generations.

Not in Webster's

Look in the dictionary, and you won't find the word "parentify." This word is forty-four-year-old Kay's, not Webster's. The oldest of three children coined it to describe what was being done to her as she was growing up. It hardly describes the soap-opera situation in which she played an unintended role. It doesn't refer to what you might suppose. For while Kay believes that helping to care for younger children is a common expectation of oldest daughters and certainly one that she experienced, "parentifying" is altogether different.

It was my responsibility to take care of my younger sisters and brother. It started when I was ten. My mother would have plans with someone, and she wouldn't want to take all of the kids. If I had plans, I had to change them to stay home and take care of the kids when she was gone. I felt two things—first, "Look how important I am" and second, "angry." I was angry because it prevented me from doing things with my friends.

When I was six years old my parents had had a party, and I saw my father kissing another woman. I told my mother because I didn't understand. She confronted him. I watched him throw a lamp, and he left. I was told it was because of me. She blamed me for her problems. When he came back, he told me he had come back because he missed me, loved me and wanted to be with me. I learned later there were many affairs.

My mother resented me, but she also needed me. I understand now. She wanted me to help take care of her emotional state. She was making me an adult. I felt some sort of equality with my parents. I didn't realize that wasn't appropriate. It's what I call parentifying. I know now that it was because my mother had no boundaries with me. I knew everything about my parents, about their relationship.

At age eighteen, I ended up in treatment and my mother was told this behavior (parentifying) was inappropriate, and so our relationship changed.

If I could give advice to parents of oldest daughters, it would be, "Let them be children."

This story speaks for itself.

Supporting Role

Ilene, forty years old, remembers her parents as "a unit. Always together. No separation."

She sees that loving relationship between her two parents as key to the bonds that were formed throughout the family. It was especially important to her in the relationship between herself, the fourth of five children, and her oldest sister.

I'm ten years younger than my sister, who is the oldest in our family. I expected her to take care of me because I was so much younger. She became like a mom to me. My mom didn't tell my sister that she expected her to take care of me. My sister took it on herself and just did it. It's her nature to be a caretaker, but also my mom taught her to be that way by example.

My sister was always there for me. I would wake up in the middle of the night and go to her room because I'd had a bad dream or something. (We were not allowed in my parents' room because of privacy.) She had a queen-size bed that was very comfortable and warm, and I always felt safe in there.

Now she supports me in everything. It doesn't matter what it is. I had twins in my first pregnancy, and I remember thinking, "I don't think I can do this." She said, "Ilene, you can do anything you put your mind to, and I'll always be there to guide you." When I came home from the hospital, she was the first one to help me, she and her kids; and I thought, "It's okay. I can do this."

Now because of what my sister has meant in my life, I tell my kids, "You're going to have a lot of people come into your lives and leave, but it's going to be your family that you'll always be able to turn to.

Ilene credits her parents with the family's ongoing close-knit adult relationships. "We enjoy taking care of each other and our families because that's what we saw when we were growing up." Since this next-to-the-youngest child in the family doesn't show or tell us about the loving, maternal things her mother did for her children, we have to take Ilene at her word that these good things happened. It is also reasonable to assume that Ilene's oldest sister modeled herself after the things she saw their mother do, perhaps for and with the older children.

Ilene obviously appreciates the nurturing her oldest sister has given her. She is grateful that this sister has continued to meet her expectations well into adulthood, supporting her "in everything." Whether as a result of their mother's or her sister's role modeling or simply doing what comes naturally, Ilene gives every indication of wanting to continue the spirit of generational mothering.

The Substitute

Memories are funny things. They often aren't about what one would expect.

When fifty-six-year-old "Rory" recalls the Christmas he was five, he doesn't mention the excitement of finding the big construction truck, toy train, scooter or anything else he might have asked for from Santa Claus that year. Instead this fifth of seven children talks about Christmas Eve. When all through the house, not a sound could be heard except that of a story being read to three small children, all cuddled together with their oldest sister.

All of the family had gone to Midnight Mass except for my oldest sister who stayed home with me and my two younger sisters. We were sitting up in my parents' bed. She was telling us the story of "The Night before Christmas." I had a sense of security, of being cared for, and of all the good warm feelings that go with Christmas.

Because there were so many children and so much upset in the family, Christmas Eve that year was one of the rare moments I had as a child for receiving attention. It is a fond and important memory.

My oldest sister was just seven years older than me, but she was essentially a stabilizing element in the family dynamic. That's because the relationship between my parents was so turbulent. They got along like cats and dogs.

My sister had a lot of responsibility. She was more or less a second mother. Just her presence created a comforting sense of security. It was like a gift because our family was fraught with volatility.

My sister was leaned on from both directions. My mother leaned on her to help with the family, and the rest of us relied on her to provide that stabilizing presence. She was the family keystone.

From what I understand in later conversations with my mother, when my sister was the only child, she and my parents were a model, functioning family. But additional children changed that. We didn't have a direct relationship with my parents because my father had backed off and become just a figurehead. And because my mother and father were constantly at each other.

So my oldest sister became the parent, the substitute mother. When I was five years old, she would take me to get my haircut, take me to the museum and so on. She was probably the most stable, maternal role model I had.

But when she was placed in charge of us, we often ignored her. Like when we were roller skating in the basement and got loud, she would tell us to be quiet. When we wouldn't, it drove her crazy.

As we got older—and especially when she was a teenager—she would say periodically that she felt imposed upon, that these weren't her *seven children. My mother resisted having my sister change her role, letting go so she could have her own friends. My mother was an oldest daughter, who had also been placed in a position to take care of her two younger sisters. That situation was more or less re-enacted from my mother to my sister.*

I appreciate what my sister did for me by stepping in as a stabilizing force in my life. I wouldn't have had much security without her care and attention, and I don't take that for granted. I feel now that it is incumbent upon me to say that. But I would like to ask her why later she felt so comfortable evaluating my life and a few years ago issuing an opinion about it. And I would like to ask her if she is aware that she was put into the role of a secondary mother and what that did to her as well as to us.

Funny what makes a stand-out memory and how it can become a stand-in for someone or something important. In the recollections of a now fifty-six-year-old man, a long-ago Christmas Eve remains as bright and clear as the night sky in the classic holiday poem his sister was reading. A memory that stands out and stands in for love and for his oldest sister. The majority of his other memories are that the anger existing between his parents resulted in family turmoil that seeped into Rory's everyday life, leaving him feeling vulnerable and impacting everyone, especially his oldest sister.

Rory needed her to create stability in the family. As an adult, he is grateful that his sister filled that role. But he recognizes the ongoing toll that being a substitute mom has taken not only on his sister but also on their relationship. A toll that could possibly create an unhappy ending to their story. She apparently has continued to assume that her "maternal" guidance is needed, while failing to recognize that it's not wanted. His questions are important if what was once special is to continue without devolving into resentment and separation.

Paying it Forward

Paula was a nineteen-year-old college student and a second-generation American when she offered to share her story. Both her parents had grown up in Eastern Europe as the functional oldests in their respective families. They met and married after each immigrated to the United States. Paula is the first-born of their four children. Both parents have always depended heavily on her to pass on whatever she learned in this new country to the three younger siblings who were very close in age to her. Paula accepted this as part of her role as the oldest daughter, though she did once ask her father, essentially—"Why am I the only one who can do this?"

I spoke Polish until I was about four years old, then learned English by myself in pre-school. I was nervous and scared, but I had been prepared by my parents to believe that I could do it.

A lot of my confidence came from the praise I got from my parents and the time they spent with me. When my siblings came along, their individual time with each of us became more and more scarce. I don't have an exact memory of what my parents said to me when my little sisters and brother were born, but my impression is that it was probably along the line of, "Here's your younger brother, your younger sister. You can help them so much. You're really the example for them."

My siblings say that more was expected of me than of them. They're aware that their childhoods were different from mine. My mom really sees me as her helping hand, and my dad looks to me if my mom's not home. I was the one helping my brother and sister with homework, the way my mom had worked with me. My dad also placed a lot of responsibility on me. He'd say, with his accent, "Come, Paula, come help your brother with his homework." Early on, my inside self might have wanted to say, "If I could do it, he could do it. I have other things to do." Sometimes I asked my father, "Why don't you ask my mom or my sister to help?" But he would insist I do it. I was his helper.

My relationship with my siblings today is positive. We're very close. I love them very, very much. With that comes a big feeling of protection.

I expect that one day there'll be a lack of hierarchy so everyone's opinion has equal value. That we'll be very friend-like. That they won't need me to look to for advice. Just a level playing field, one person asking of another person, no sense of duty.

Being the oldest daughter really puts you into a pseudo-maternal role your whole life. You're constantly seeing everything from a protective point of view. I could see the way my mother loved her children. I would do things that mimicked her, and I was encouraged to do so. I don't think I ever resented doing that. It makes me who I am today. It's a lot easier to adapt to situations or see things from a different point of view because I had that maternal lens to use throughout my childhood.

I see myself getting married someday and having children. As much as I did for my siblings, I'll be able to carry that on to my children.

Paula could easily be a persuasive spokesperson for the "pay it forward" movement—first passing on to her siblings the benefits she received from her parents and then planning to give her future family the values and practices she garnered from her family of origin.

She credits her parents' examples for her desire to do this. They did not expect anything more of their oldest child and first-born female than they had already given of themselves to her.

The vision Paula has of her future relationships with her siblings is worth noting. She looks forward to a time with her siblings when they will be more like peers.

Whether her goal will be realized will depend not only on her continued determination to have the relationship she describes. It will also hinge on the willingness of her siblings in the future to change the way they see her. Will they want to stop regarding her as the secondary mother they have always experienced? Or, as adults, will they recognize the value she describes in being part of a "level playing field" of friends?

Professional Insight

Successful family functioning usually requires older children to assume responsibilities that younger children are not yet capable of. Families generally function by having everyone do what they are able to do in order to meet daily household demands.

However, it is also important for parents to encourage younger children as they become older and more capable to share those responsibilities *and* for parents not to expect older children to perform adult tasks. Appropriate delegation of tasks to children may not happen if parents are overwhelmed or if they believe the oldest children should help parent.

As difficult as this can be, it is imperative that parents do their best NOT to place parental roles on children, unless it is absolutely necessary.

It is terrifying for children when a parent isn't taking care of things. Children know someone has to take care of things. They intuitively know when adults are not capable of handling situations or that nobody's running the show. What usually ends up happening when the oldest or most responsible child sees, "this isn't working," is that this child develops coping skills to meet the need or avert the crisis.

So sometimes—especially in crisis situations—an older child may be taking on responsibilities that realistically belong to parents. Unfortunately, some circumstances in life point families in this direction (e.g., when one parent dies).

Too often parents fall prey to doing what is easiest. This may result in asking older children to take on more than they should—being overly responsible for younger children and/or no longer being adequately parented, especially in the teenage years.

Many oldest daughters were taught, whether directly or indirectly, that they were responsible for helping with younger children. In some situations they felt, and may still feel, that they are to function in a parenting role.

For Reflection:

- *What do I want my relationships with my family-of-origin members to be?*
- *Am I choosing the role I have for myself, or am I trying to meet someone else's expectations of me?*

Kristin S. Russell, Ph.D.

A 'no' uttered from deepest conviction is better and greater than a 'yes' merely uttered to please

Attributed to Mahatma Gandhi

Chapter 5.

Response-Ability

I was feeling hurt. When my mother had described me as sometimes being bossy (shared in Chapter 3.), I had wanted to blurt out, "Mom, you are responsible for much of the way I am today." Fortunately, I did not. I mentally repeated a prayer line I often say to myself. "Let me not seek so much to be understood as to understand."

She spoke next, still without opening her eyes and in an even softer tone of voice. "Sometimes I think I put too much responsibility on you."

I was totally caught off guard. Without knowing it, my cherished mother had hit on the survey word oldest daughters most often select to describe themselves

Responsible.

I was beginning to understand that she didn't mean what I—and I would bet a lot of other oldest daughters—think of when that word is used. What Mom was trying to say was not that she'd put too much responsibility on me over the years for my younger siblings. But that now, she was afraid she was putting too much responsibility on me *for herself!*

Her words were in reaction to her sense that she had unintentionally given away the ability to make her own choices by giving me responsibility for her medical decisions. Simply put, she had expected to be supported, not dictated to. The unexpected "bossiness" she saw in me resulted largely from the responsibility I felt for ensuring her well-being. I had not been sensitive to the reality that in wanting to do the best for my mother, I had inadvertently played into the control game. I determined to become more mindful of my own future words and actions.

The way Mom described me in refusing to take her shower never came up again between us. But a few weeks later, an ironic incident occurred.

I was listed in the nursing home's records as having power of attorney for her health care. In doing a periodic review, an administrator had given Mom the choice to either maintain or change this. "Your mother was adamant," she told me later. "She wanted no one but you to do this." Apparently my mother saw this as "Good Responsibility," not "Bossy."

Of course, I told the administrator, I'd be happy to continue.

At the same time, however, I was becoming aware that the growing list of requirements for Mom's care was creating a different challenge. I was straining to find time and energy to respond to the important, ongoing needs of my husband and family, my job and myself.

I asked my next-in-line sibling. "Can't you see that such and such needs to be done for Mom and that I can't do it all?" Her response was almost as unsettling as Mom's remarks had been a few weeks earlier. "Sure, but why should I offer to help? You're going to do it your way anyway." Gulp.

Her blunt comment could explain, in part at least, my siblings' reluctance or even resistance to step up and help. But... I felt they didn't see all the things that needed to be done for Mom. Why would they? Those things were being taken care of. To quote the words of Tiffany in Chapter 1., "If I'm going to be doing it all, why should they get a clue? They don't need to."

So how would I respond to this new realization? Obviously I had to take a different approach.

I started by regularly voicing a list of Mom's current needs and then asking for specific help to meet them. Making this change opened the door to cooperation but also created some immediate discomfort and protests. I tried to listen not only to the words being spoken but also to hear the unspoken words, the feelings.

When I talked, I began intentionally developing a softer, warmer tone of voice. I became more willing to consider alternative solutions, including that not all Mom's needs required immediate attention. Initially that was uncomfortable for me and brought out my own objections.

Over time strategic collaboration between me and my siblings increased. Rivulets of resentment, previously unacknowledged on all sides, gradually dried up. I also experienced more free time.

Response-ability.

To suggest that "all a person has to do is make up her mind to change the way she responds" would be unrealistic. It would do a disservice to those individuals whose opportunities for change are limited by family circumstances or attitudes or for whom no options seem good. An oldest daughter's sense of family responsibility is determined by many things, not the least of which are the expectations still in her that had been instilled in her long ago.

This chapter is about how other oldest daughters have chosen to respond to demanding situations in their lives—and the subsequent results.

Other R Words

Thirty-nine-year-old Kelly grew up as the oldest of three children. Both parents had high expectations for her from the get-go. Her mother, who was herself an oldest daughter, expected Kelly to repeat the experience of "basically raising" younger siblings. Her father pushed his oldest child to excel in all aspects of her life. Kelly exercised the ability to choose how she would respond to these expectations.

I had a huge amount of responsibility at a young age. When my brothers were children, I was responsible for making them go to bed and follow rules. When we were teenagers, my parents were gone all the time. I didn't know any better—I was happy they'd be out of town. I was responsible for making sure everything was okay at our house.

My father influenced me a great deal in terms of thought process. He was extremely competitive and successful. I think he saw in me what he saw in himself.

My mother was an oldest daughter. My life was harder because of that. She was the oldest of six. She had raised her brothers and had had a huge amount of responsibility. She passed that on to me. By the time I was able to take care of my brothers, she was basically hands off. I made all the decisions for myself, and my brothers followed. I definitely influenced the direction of my brothers. My middle brother probably resents that tremendously.

As a mom and a wife and with business colleagues and friends, I have this same role. My husband, an oldest son, says I'm the decision-maker. I see myself as a leader. I definitely take the initiative. My dad raised me that way. I'm not the mousy type. I'm always going to put in my two cents, and I tend to sway the group in my direction. I suppose my tone of voice is part of that, so I hope it's not shrill. I'm always aggressive-aggressive, not passive-aggressive. It's self- assurance.

I've been described at the office as a whirling dervish, running circles around other people in the amount of work I can get done. I've always had my hands in different things. My friends describe me as holding a baby in one arm, on speaker phone selling stocks and cooking dinner—all at the same time.

Confidence comes from within. It has to be built. It's not necessarily innate. There's no "automatic confidence." It comes from responsibilities and successes.

During our interview Kelly described the difference that responsibility has made in her life and her mother's.

"I had certain expectations of my mother as a grandmother. But she will not have any responsibilities for grandchildren. She loves being a grandmother, but wants hands off. She doesn't want responsibilities."

In her own life, Kelly has made different choices. Continuing to meet, rather than evade, responsibility has enabled her to confidently fill the multiple roles she desires as wife, mother, and professional. The Rewards of Response-ability.

Destiny's script

"Responsibility stops here" could be twenty-five-year-old Rhoda's mantra. She grew up as the oldest daughter in a family of four siblings. Responsibility is something she's always been used to, though at times it has been overwhelming. Now the mother of her own four children, ages two months to eight years, she continues to accept it as part of her role in life.

Rhoda's tone is part apologetic, part defensive as she begins to speak. The story she tells illustrates that she doesn't expect the same level of responsibility from her younger siblings that she does from herself. The tone of her voice changes when she explains why.

My sister who's right next to me had a son when she was nineteen. She really wasn't ready to be a mother yet. She still wanted to be young and go out and party.

I had two children by that time. I offered to take care of her son, to raise him in my family. After a couple of years of struggle, she kind of stepped up to the plate and started doing her role. But for two years I kept him during the day and our mother kept him at night. I didn't resent it. I felt it was my place to do that.

I think that's why I'm the oldest child, because of my personality, of who I am. I believe that's who God made me to be. I wouldn't change it for anything. It makes me feel good to be that person. It makes me feel like I'm needed, valued.

Rhoda's story calls attention to an important point. This chapter isn't meant to suggest one-size-fits-all response-ability. It's commonly accepted that people change their behaviors when what is happening in their lives makes them uncomfortable enough to do so. Rhoda is not uncomfortable. She says point blank that she wouldn't change "for anything."

Her voice shrugs as she explains what that means going forward. "We oldest daughters spend so many years worrying and thinking about our siblings, I don't think we can shut it off once we become adults."

Wish List

In her professional life, twenty-six-year-old Leigh works with children. She believes her responsibilities growing up as the oldest of five sisters have given her definite advantages. "You learn to deal with a bunch of different personalities and how personalities work. You learn to live with other people. I feel like I'm a pretty good judge of character, good at listening, even reading between the lines."

In her personal life, however, there are some oldest-daughter responsibilities she wishes were truly different.

I think people treat you different, have different expectations when you're the oldest.

Growing up I was very assertive and kind of bossy, directing everyone which way to go. In a way, I was kind of the second mother. None of my other sisters felt that way, but they would all agree that's who I was.

I liked not being bossed around by somebody else, but the responsibility was hard. At the time, speaking in my head to my mom, I thought, "This is not my problem, this is your problem." I don't know if I ever said it aloud to her. When I was mad, I would be very cautious about how I said things.

But it's not the same for my next sister in line. She's very independent, at a totally different end of the spectrum. When I left for college, she called and said, "I hate this. I hate the responsibility. I want you to come home." And I think she actually said this to my mom when she had to babysit. My mom told me she told her, "Your sister would never have said that."

I don't push the envelope like my younger sisters do. All my mother has to do is raise her eyebrows, and I'm right back on course. If I'd pushed the envelope, repercussions might have been worse because I have these younger sisters I was supposed to be setting example for.

I never was very kid-like. I was pretty grown up right from the beginning. All my family would say that. Part personality, part my place in the family. If anybody said, "I need you," I would be there for them. I like to be needed. That is the role I've always had.

I wish I could let others do their part and not feel that I need to do it.

I wish I could be more carefree because I think it would be more pleasurable for myself and everyone else. But I don't feel as purposeful or productive if I'm not busy.

I wish my sisters were a little more perceptive of my needs. But I don't need them to take care of me. I don't want someone to be overly attentive, but I'd like for someone to listen to what I'm saying. Really listen. To really hear what I'm saying so they can better understand what my reaction would be.

I might ask them to take on a little more responsibility. It doesn't cross their minds to do it for me. And that's disappointing. They never think, "Leigh would want this."

There are a lot of "wishes" in Leigh's story, not the least of which are the desires to get to a more carefree place and to have her own needs recognized. But how does an oldest daughter, brought up to be *responsible* do this?

I once asked a specialist in family-systems theory this same question. I thought he was pulling my leg when he responded, "Hire one of her siblings as a coach." But he wasn't kidding. He suggested that an oldest daughter who would like to lighten up say to a younger sister or brother, "I don't know how to play. I need your help."

What a twist. The oldest sister asking a sibling for help *for herself.* Asking for, not giving, personal advice. Not just wishing things would somehow change.

Almost five hundred years ago the Scottish people recorded the proverb, "If wishes were horses, beggars would ride." Those kilt-clad folks spoke a pocketful of wisdom. Don't rely on wishes to get you where you want to go.

More recently the Golden Rule has advised, "Do unto others as you would have them do unto you." It's the last part of that sentence that is problematic, just as Leigh pointed out. Others don't always think of what you would want. Unless you let them know.

Response-ability. For all in the family.

Professional Insight

I often hear women describe themselves as people pleasers—those who do things so someone else is happy or okay with them.

I believe that most women can benefit from learning to tolerate the uncomfortable feelings that occur when another person is not all right with their choices. When women are able to do this, they can then be responsible for taking steps towards their own happiness.

If oldest daughters have been put in the role of having more responsibility and doing more than others in the family, it is important as adults to assess whether they want to continue to function in this capacity. If they don't make conscious choices about what roles and responsibilities they want to continue to meet, they risk becoming resentful and not recognizing their own power to decide what they do and don't want to take on. It is also important for them to realize that others may not like or want to accept the changes they are making.

In addition, adults who are also parents need to decide how they want to bring up their own children. It is up to every parent to be aware of her/his varying expectations. Do mothers and fathers want to teach their oldest daughter and her siblings that she has different expectations than others in the family? Parents who don't increase age-appropriate responsibilities for all their children fail to give them equal opportunities to develop age-appropriate skills.

It is critical that parents ask, "Whose needs are being served when I ask a child to take on more responsibility?" Obviously, there are situations in which all children have to be more responsible, such as when only one parent is present or available and/or when both parents are overburdened.

Slowly exposing children to more responsibilities so they can become independent, learn how to manage crisis, develop coping skills, etc. is healthy. It can become unhealthy when parents are capable of doing things themselves, but routinely ask a child to take on a task simply to give themselves a break.

A child who is expected or required to take on too many responsibilities at a young age can experience negatives such as loss of "childhood" and an ability to be more carefree. Such expectations could also be why many oldest daughters I've observed describe themselves as not knowing how to have fun.

For Reflection:

Did I have more responsibility in the house or for my siblings than other children in my family? If so, did my siblings also have to do more as they became older?

- ☐ *As an adult, do my parents still expect me to do more? Do my siblings expect so also?*
- ☐ *If I am expected to be more responsible for my parents or siblings than other family members, do I willingly accept this responsibility?*
- ☐ *If not, have I ever addressed the situation or expressed how I feel with my family?*
- ☐ *What might the consequences be for me if I did?*

Kristin S. Russell, Ph.D.

"You can hardly make a friend in a year, but you can lose one in an hour."

Chinese Proverb

Chapter 6.

Siblingspeak

No picture of an oldest daughter would be complete—or fair—without the input of those persons who lived most closely with her as they were all growing up. So in interviews and online surveys, I asked siblings to share their feelings and memories.

- *What do they most remember about her?*
- *What impact has she had on their lives?*
- *Do they think being the oldest daughter is any big deal?*
- *Is her position any different from any other in the family?*

The many-sided picture of the oldest daughter that emerges from sibling stories and comments is like a Picasso painting. Admired often. Not always pretty or easy to look at.

In this chapter I have made every effort to exclude any aspect of my "oldest-daughter" self that might add an unintentional brushstroke to someone else's painting. Therefore, the only words that are mine in the next several pages are in the introduction to each person's story as a way of providing a framework.

The Driver's Seat

"Sarah" is not an oldest daughter. She is the third child and second daughter in a family of six children. Because she was only two years younger than the first-born female in her family, many of the expectations for the two girls were ostensibly the same.

But what happens when the one who is the oldest daughter chronologically exhibits more authority and power than the second in command? How does this affect their relationship? What's a girl to do when an oldest daughter learns that making others uncomfortable gets her what she wants?

Those are the circumstances Sarah found herself in when she was growing up and now says she has had trouble outgrowing.

My older sister has a domineering personality. She's a take-charge person and a perfectionist. It's always been her way or no way.

She always got to sit in the front seat of our green station wagon. She was the oldest. It was her position. We thought it was unfair, but she was bigger than we were.

I wondered how she knew what to do, but she always acted like somehow she knew. She also told me what I was to do.

My sister had the attitude that whatever she said was right and whatever she wanted done, you did. She was older, so I just assumed that's the way it was supposed to be. Even when there were other choices, I chose to do what she did.

If she got upset when we were growing up, it intimidated me even more than if my parents did. She had more access to me than my parents. We had the same bedroom, went to the same school. I believe she was deliberately controlling. I'm pretty sure she knew what she was doing.

If we had to do dishes or clean up, she was the dictator. She would tell each person what they needed to do. We actually called her The Second Mom. She had more responsibilities, of course. She took over when she needed to, making sure things got done. When my younger sister was born, my mom was not ready to take care of another baby, and my older sister and I were basically the moms for the first year. She was ten; I was eight. Taking care of the little ones was given to both of us, but that didn't make us close because I had to do what she told me to do.

I was a follower. That's just the way it was. She was the boss. I don't think I ever thought about whether she'd like to do something else besides be the second mom. I don't think she was given a choice.

I don't think it ever entered my mind to expect anything of myself with regard to her when we were growing up.

Now I expect her to understand that I am no longer a child and shouldn't have to bow to her every wish even though most of my family does anyway.

I would like her to think I'm successful and treat me as an adult. She does for the most part, but when she wants something from you, she's not afraid to ask. She's also not afraid to manipulate. If you can accommodate her, then she's happy. But when I have told her that I can't do what she wants, she gets upset and generally I feel guilty. I don't like it when she gets upset. You don't piss her off—that's the way it's always been.

As an adult, I do expect myself to stand up to her and to have her follow my wishes, but I generally cave in to what her wishes are. I think I allow myself to be a "victim." It's my choice, but it makes me angry. I guess the deal is I don't like confrontation, so it's better to do what she's asking.

When Push Comes to Shove

Forty-five-year-old Leonard grew up sandwiched between two sisters. From many males' perspective, this would be an unenviable position—especially having a sister as "the first." Not so for Leonard. When he was born, she was already three years old. By the time they were both in elementary school, that age difference provided him with an advantage he enjoyed and used. Until one day he made a big mistake.

My life would be very different if not for my oldest sister. For one thing, I probably would have been beat up about five hundred times.

She walked me to school, made sure I got there. She wasn't like a mother. She was like my protector. I relished having her stick up for me.

From second through fifth grades, I kind of used her. I'd set up scenarios where I knew she would protect me. Like with one guy who was a little overweight. I teased him, so he started chasing me around. I ended up telling my sister, and she whomped on him because she thought he had harmed me.

She'd always err on the side of protecting me instead of doubting me. She never put me through the "cry-wolf" syndrome. It's part of the security I felt.

Until I turned sixteen or so, she was taller than me, lean and athletic. But I was never afraid of her. I was always very comfortable with her. But once I got too comfortable. I can still see us. (Laugh)

I was around eleven years old and we were outside. The night before my sister had had a sleepover with her friends. I had harassed them, not letting them sleep. She asked me why I had done that. I told her, "I can do what I want, I can beat you up." That was my mistake. She was into judo. She flipped me around a few times. My neighbors were watching and they really razzed me about it!

My sister was the smart one, the wise one. I did okay. There's never been any rivalry. She helped me look up to her instead of competing with her.

Now we live half a continent apart, but we're still close. That's through her efforts. I'm the one who moved far away. But she continued to keep in communication with me. She always sent me something for holidays like Kwanzaa and for special events.

That's been important because it showed she really loved me as a brother. It wasn't just talk. What she did demonstrated how important it is to keep the bond we had. I thought this was really great and decided that I can do it, too. It has grown into something very special for us as adults.

Without her, our relationship wouldn't be as in-depth as it is now. It's not just, "Hi, how are you?" We can end up talking for hours. She makes it easy to say what I really feel. I like this accepted openness.

Oldest sisters have a role that is special and different from others. They have to be willing to set the example as someone responsible and to embrace that.

I've been blessed to have that kind of sister. I'll always love her. Always.

Whoever Has the Voice

In a review of the London musical, *Matilda,* Ben Brantley *New York Times* Theatre Reviewer, described one of the play's morals this way: "Who owns the language has the power." Thirty-six-year old "Lauren" gets that. She just says it a little differently. Whoever has the voice, has the power.

During most of her childhood, her voice was "the second to be heard." If it was heard at all. That's because her older sister and only sibling literally always spoke first. Lauren doesn't describe any impaired vocal chords or lung capacity to explain why she couldn't speak. Things might have continued that way had fate not stepped up to the mike.

My sister is four and a half years older. She was always the leader. Perhaps I didn't feel like I had a voice. She was the voice of the two of us until I was about seven and started saying some words on my own. When she was twelve, my sister became very ill and was hospitalized and so she couldn't speak for us. That's when I began to really use my own voice.

Because of her illness she went to a private middle school. I went to a public school. So I had a fresh set of teachers and people who didn't know my sister. I was able to continue using my voice. I was able to be me.

Before that, I had to fit into her mold. Perhaps my sister expected me a little bit to be like her, but it was primarily others. Teachers in our small community—elementary school especially—as well as other people who knew her, expected me to be like her. And they would tell me I wasn't. I was actually a little better student but a little more mischievous than she was. It could be I knew I could not live up to that well-behaved expectation, so I just didn't bother trying.

If I could change anything—maybe as a child I would have spoken up for myself more and made some of my own decisions. Most often she did both. (Laugh) She had the power, you know. Being the younger one and a much smaller child, I didn't have the same capabilities. I wasn't able to articulate for myself. She did that for me. It became expected.

After we became adults, early on she tried to continue speaking for me, particularly when I was going through a difficult period in my life. When I was trying to find a job or was in a relationship crisis, she would take on a motherly kind of role, telling me what to do or what I should say. On the one hand, it was comforting. But I wanted to say, "Mind your own business. I'm an adult now. I can speak for myself."

I've probably never told her that. I may have made it known to her through body language or by not calling her, but I never came out with the words.

Actually she listens to me now, for the most part. We are more like peers. There's more of a mutuality to our relationship, so I don't expect her to be "the voice."

I value her ability to stand up for herself. I have that now, more so than I did as a child.

Words of Mouth

"Sticks and stones may break my bones, but words will never hurt me."

It's a common childhood sing-song, a retort to a playground taunt. But in the experience of "Charlotte," age twenty-six, this verbal pushback is neither honest nor effective. She has one sibling, a sister who's three and a-half- years older. When they were growing up, that sister didn't do anything physically to hurt Charlotte. Instead, she created emotional wounds by taunting and getting others to join in the harassment.

What is a younger sibling to do when an older sister seems to be just plain mean? What would it take to change things between them? To change her?

Whether or not her sister knew the effect she was having on Charlotte at the time, she knows now. When she became an adult, Charlotte confronted her.

When you're a child, you're not equipped to deal with a relationship that's difficult. Growing up, my connection with my sister was not very good.

She was a mean kid. She was very much about having friends from school and church kind of gang up on me, say inappropriate things and be mean. Usually she caused the situation. Nobody ever really came up and bullied me on her own. It was always my sister and her friends.

It started when I was ten and she was thirteen. We were at school waiting for a ride. All of her friends were hanging out, and she and they started calling me "Baby." I tried to walk away, but they followed me because they thought it was okay. A little later on, the name calling became about my weight. I felt humiliated because other kids could hear.

I couldn't talk to her. I waited till I got home and talked to my parents. Their response was not what I wanted. They sat her down and said, "You shouldn't do that. It's not nice."

There was nothing to stop her from doing this. She'd say, "What's going to happen? They're going to talk to me again?"

Our parents had the same expectations of both of us. I've always been pretty self-sufficient. They didn't think she needed to be my protector.

My sister never tried to control me by saying things like, "You can't borrow clothes" or anything like that. Instead, she would want to take control of a situation, to make herself look like a hotshot in front of people. Possibly it also gave her some power over me. But I don't have a weak personality. I would yell back at her. I never said mean things, but I was very vocal. I would try to get away from her, but she would follow me. I would have hoped that she would have been more protecting instead of leaving me exposed.

I recall wishing as a child that she wouldn't do those things. I remember asking her why she did them. I think she usually said, "I don't know." Once she actually said, "It was fun," or that she liked getting a rise out of me.

Even as an adult, it's pretty easy for her to get a reaction from me. It used to be a daily thing. Maybe she does it once a year now—teases about something. I'll think, "I've already had this ten years ago, why are you doing it again?"

Three or four years ago she came to visit me and—I don't know why I did it—I sat down and told her, "I want to let you know some of the things you did when we were kids. I don't know if you know that it affected me then and affects me now. I don't think I have the most positive image of myself because of that."

She seemed very shocked and said she was very sorry, that she didn't mean for me to feel that way. But in the back of my mind then, I thought maybe she was sorry just because she thought it was the right thing to say.

Our relationship has changed now. She's done a complete one-eighty. Her demeanor changed after she got married and had a child last year. I spent the first week with her. It was a wonderful week. She needed my help. It was a bonding experience for both of us. I value her friendship now.

She is expecting her second child. I'll probably tell her, "Don't let your children treat each other the way you treated me. Because the feelings stay with you even after you're an adult."

Wave Runner

Fifty-one-year-old Mark is the first-born male and the second child in his family. He is two years younger than his sister, the family's first-born female and the oldest child. Their father's expectation that Mark, his older sister and their two younger siblings would follow traditional ethnic and family customs was set early on. That was the assumption.

The reality brought home to their father by his first-born child was something "very" (a word Mark used frequently during the interview for emphasis) different and caused ripples if not waves.

My dad's parents came to the U.S. before my dad was born. He was a first-generation American from a very old-world family.

I remember my sister would always stand up for her rights, which was very against the norm for my dad's family.

After a big family meal with all the cousins, the men would go off by themselves. But my older sister was very independent. She would not stay in her gender-designated area, the kitchen, where all the aunts and girl cousins were. She would come into the living room and try to participate in conversations. It was very awkward for my dad. He would say to her, "This is not for you." She would mind him, but she'd made her point.

I got to see this. I thought she was nuts to stand up to dad. He was raised very old world. I was smarter than that. I stayed behind the scene. I spoke when spoken to. My sister spoke up. She was courageous.

When we were growing up, my dad had lesser expectations of her as far as business was concerned, but more expectations of her around the home. Because that's what girls did then.

My sister's role was supposed to be female-oriented. She excelled in what she did. She sewed and was very good at it. That was a girl thing. She did not participate in sports. My mom expected her to help all the time. Her role was to watch over us, her younger brothers and sister. I knew that was her role. I thought it was reasonable. That's the way it was with the families in the neighborhood in which the oldest was a girl. They, too, would keep an eye on their brothers. That was the norm at the time.

If I'd been born first, my sister would have been in charge of the two younger ones, not me. As it was, she was in charge of all of us. I wasn't in charge of anyone. But even as kids and as I got older, it was my responsibility to protect my sister. Absolutely I felt that. I still feel that way.

I expect professionalism from my sister. I expect her to succeed in whatever she does. To be at the top. We were all taught, "Don't settle for mediocrity." You have to strive all the time to be above most. She did that. She was a good example for me. She inspired me to succeed. She's committed to whatever she does, one hundred percent. That's what I value most about her. She doesn't do anything half-way. She jumps in head-first and goes.

She's excelled in business. I think dad was more proud of her accomplishments because he hadn't expected that much. He was raised ethnically. He had two brothers and one sister. All the males were in the business. His sister was not.

As I've gotten older, I have more respect for her. Nothing has changed. She still strives to be the best. She's right up front. Forward. Outgoing. No one's going to hold her down. I still absolutely admire that. We're all very proud of what she's done.

Little Things

Sometimes it's those little things. Annoyances. What's said. What's not said. Little things that can chip away at a relationship until it barely exists. Once in a while, it's also a "little thing" that can rejuvenate that connection. At age twenty-nine, Jeremy has experienced both types with his older sister. They are the two oldest children in their family. There is one younger brother. It is the connection, or lack of it, with his older sister, that has most concerned Jeremy as an adult.

Except for some mild antagonism, I don't honestly recall interacting much with my sister after the age of nine or ten. Once she became a pre-teen she was off doing her stuff. When she was in high school, our relationship grew into a decent amount of animosity.

We shared a car for two years in high school. It was probably the worst thing that ever happened to us. She used to make me ride in the back seat, even if there was nobody in the front seat. She had the car all to herself. She had the high school all to herself for two years, and then she had to share it. That's probably what drove me to the "I'm going to be different than my sister" place. And then she left for college.

One very fateful Thanksgiving dinner we both stormed off. I don't remember what it was about. I would spout off about something. She would about something else. Sibling rivalry at its worse. I just remember feeling very uncomfortable. It was never resolved in any formal way. One of the many things we just let hang there.

I don't really know my sister that well anymore, and she doesn't know me. In the eleven years since we've lived in the same house, there have been periods in our adult lives when we went as long as three years without talking to each other. There was a lot of animosity. Some of that has healed over as we've both grown, but I don't know if we've spent enough time together for a relationship to really form.

I'm glad that I don't feel there's any ill will between us anymore. Occasionally when people speak of closeness to their siblings, I wish we had that. I don't think there's any sibling rivalry now. At least not on my end. She's very successful. And when I graduated and got a good job, I think I probably thought it's all even now.

I think my sister's role as the oldest daughter affected me more than I ever would have admitted. It's interesting and hard for me to characterize. I've met oldest daughters who were caretakers. That was never my experience. She's a very strong person. I've only begun to understand that. The strength she has always shown, even if I did occasionally think it was misguided, has been influential.

I don't feel like I know her anymore and I would like to. I'd probably most like to say a very genuine, "I love you," because I don't know if that's ever been said.

Every time we've been together, it hasn't seemed appropriate. We never had heart-to-heart talks in our family. It just wasn't done. Now it's a little awkward. We just don't do it. I wouldn't mind if our relationship were a little closer. I wish we had that.

I do hope things may change. My wife and I have a two-year-old son, and my sister likes my son. She was pleased when I called and asked her to be guardian of our son if anything happened to my wife and me. She didn't even hesitate. It was actually a nice moment between us. That seems to have increased our involvement somewhat.

I love my sister dearly and hope good things for her, but it's difficult. I'm sure we would be closer if we lived closer together. I don't expect her to be overly involved in my life or vice versa. My main concern is that we maintain a connection so that my son knows who his aunt and uncle are, who his family is. Family is really important.

Professional Insight

There are times when we don't recognize, or perhaps would rather not hear, the way our voices come across to others—the tones we use when defensive or exasperated or the feelings we generate and then attempt to improve by saying "I didn't mean it that way."

If an oldest daughter is taking an authoritative position, does everyone understand and accept it's because that is her role? If so, communicating from this clear position shouldn't be a problem. However, if she is interacting with adult siblings who do not see her as an authority, she may want to learn communication skills that do not convey dominance.

For Reflection by an oldest daughter's siblings:

- ☐ *Did I perceive my oldest sister as being responsible for me growing up? If so, how did this affect our relationship at the time?*
- ☐ *What are my expectations of her now? Are they different than those I have of my other siblings?*
- ☐ *If my oldest sister offers unwanted advice, have I considered why she does this?*

- ☐ *Have I ever talked to her about how I feel when she does this?*
- ☐ *Whose needs were being served when our parents asked the oldest daughter (or any siblings) to take on more responsibility?*
- ☐ *Growing up, did you feel family responsibilities were fairly divided?*
- ☐ *Looking back, do you believe your oldest sister generally had more responsibilities than you did? If so, how do you feel about that now?*
- ☐ *Did all of us eventually get the message that everyone is expected to share family responsibilities? That responsibilities prepare you for independence?*

Kristin S. Russell, Ph.D.

A son is a son til he takes him a wife
A daughter's a daughter all of her life
Anonymous

Chapter 7.

Ties that Bind

I am an oldest daughter married to a youngest son. How common is that? I have no scientific statistics about the pairing of spouses by birth order, but I did have an experience that even now seems remarkable.

A few years ago I attended a holiday open house hosted by a business colleague with whom I was newly acquainted. By the time I got to her home most of the guests had left, but several people remained in the kitchen, seated around a farmhouse-style pine table.

When she introduced me, the hostess mentioned that I was in the process of writing a book about oldest daughters. The guests' more-than-usual interest took me aback until she explained that the women gathered there—herself, her daughter, sister-in-law and three cousins—were all oldest daughters. The ensuing conversation then revealed that except for the teenage daughter, each woman, including myself, was married to a youngest son. What were the chances?

At the time this happened, my husband and I belonged to a social group that had been meeting weekly for a few years. I knew that most of the wives happened to be oldest daughters and I thought several of the husbands were youngest sons. So I decided to share my holiday incident with this group. I ended with, "I wonder why oldest-daughter/youngest-son marriages seem to be so common.

A Cheshire grin crept across the face of one of the husbands as he responded, "Youngest sons grow up hearing their oldest sisters give orders. Then we let what they said roll off our backs. That's why marriages between youngest sons and oldest daughters work so well!" His comment was met with chuckles and whoops.

I pushed on. "What about marriages between oldest sons and oldest daughters? How do they fare?"

One wife spoke up, "It can be difficult when you're both used to being the decision-maker." And her husband added, "We both understand our sense of responsibility, especially to our families." Then he speculated, "But if both oldests have very strong personalities, it could be a problem. There would have to be compromise, and compromise in our culture is not common."

I considered my own marriage. No doubt there's truth to the adage, "opposites attract." [2] As an oldest daughter, I tend to be more serious. Rob loved to laugh and did so frequently at things he found genuinely humorous. One characteristic of my personality type[3] "The Romantic Idealist," is intensity. Rob was laid-back and could indeed let things roll off his back. This yin/yang together with the important values we held in common proved invaluable for us.

As I mentioned, I don't have any scientific facts and figures about birth-order marriages. Nor do I have any data from my survey. I had failed to ask, "What is the birth-order position of your spouse?" That detail in hindsight would have been useful. However, the information often came out spontaneously in interviews.

In talking with individuals of both genders, I realized that nowhere is the word "expectations" more laden with hope, frustration, disappointment or fulfillment than in spousal relationships. These interviews confirmed that we don't see ourselves as others, even our spouses, see us.

This chapter can act like a virtual mirror, reflecting the feelings and observations of individuals who either

---

[2] In the intro to Chapter 3 I mentioned my high school homeroom election in which a super-nice guy was chosen as leader with me as co-leader. Turns out he is a youngest son. The saying has it that politics makes strange bedfellows. The same might be said of marriages.

[3] See Resources, Enneagram

married an oldest daughter or are themselves oldest daughters who've experienced marriage. The "takeaway" from each story depends on if/what each reader sees in the storyteller's mirror.

The men who tell their stories over the next several pages were interviewed because they had identified themselves as "spouse" on the survey or in an email. Each speaks about how his wife's position in her family of origin has affected their marriage. Each also offers opinions about the advantages or disadvantages of being married to a woman who is a first-born female and sometimes also an oldest child.

The oldest daughters in this chapter were not originally interviewed because of their marital status. However at some point each had mentioned the role her husband's birth-order position had played in their marriages.

Both husbands and wives were candid about how their spouse's place in his/her family of origin affects those they love—and who love them—in this most intimate, important family relationship.

For better or "worser."

In the Name of Love

Twenty-seven-year-old Michael and his twenty-four-year-old wife met, fell in love, and married when they were still college undergraduates. After three years of marriage, they are now the parents of a two-year-old daughter and a three-month-old baby girl. Michael is also finishing a degree program.

No surprise that with their parenting/student/work schedules stress has come into their married life. The surprise, for Michael at least, was the source of the stress.

We were married for a little more than two years when because my wife was homesick, we moved back to the city where her parents lived.

Her parents don't ask her for assistance. It's her siblings.

Her younger siblings and even her older brother all treat her as a second mother. They expect her to help them with their problems. Everything from marital difficulties to grammar. That takes time and energy and creates stress. She is glad to do that. But because she has so many siblings, she resents when they come to her too often. They are old enough to appreciate that she has a lot of other things on her plate, but they don't take that into consideration.

She has never said anything to them about this. She sometimes gave hints, but she thought it was her place to help them. My best guess is that she created this idea herself. She's done this since she was young. She just grew up with this. She expects, and they expect her, to be there for them when they need her even if she's busy with something else. They don't have the same expectations for each other.

I'd like them to ask my wife if she has the time to help. That would be a nice courtesy which doesn't happen. I would like her to stand up more for herself, and I have told her this. She says it would just become something else she has to do. That it's basically not a big deal. Generally, that would be correct. But she's also very kind-hearted, and I don't think she'd ever be bold enough to say something.

It's hard to tell if things will get easier when her siblings have their own families. I think that if they live very close, it would continue to be a problem. I want them to live a little distance away to create their own families.

Ultimately I think she will have to be the one to set the boundaries.

The biggest advantage of being married to an oldest daughter is that she probably has developed a kind heart, wants to help, thinks of others. That's a great trait. The biggest disadvantage is that if you have a big family, it can take too much away from her own time and needs.

What advice would I give other males regarding marriage to an oldest daughter? If there is too much interference, then politely tell the family that your wife needs to take a break. And then be an advocate for her.

In my online survey the word "caring" was chosen by siblings as the word they would say best describes their oldest sister. I didn't ask oldest daughters, siblings or spouses any questions about boundaries. In hindsight, doing so could have proven beneficial.

Unexpected Inheritance

Asked to describe himself, sixty-four-year-old John comes up with a long list. Black male born in southern Arkansas. Former grave digger. Shoe shiner. Cook. Worker in the garment-industry. Machinist for twenty-five years. These *describe* him, he says. What *defines* him is his marriage thirty-seven years ago to his second, and current, wife. She is an oldest daughter. He maintains that her birth-order position has changed his life.

I met my wife on a blind date. She wasn't like the girls I'd formerly dated. She was more reserved and wasn't willing to do all the things I wanted to do. I drank, gambled, did young persons' stuff. She wasn't a club-hopper like I was. She was somebody I could talk to.

I'd probably known her about six months when I found out she was the oldest daughter. It didn't really mean anything to me at the time.

After we'd been dating for a couple of years, I went home with her for a visit. That's when I first realized what it meant. She had six sisters. There were six years between her and the next sister. The rest were all two years apart. All of the little sisters were waiting to meet her boyfriend. They wanted her to tell them about her experiences in the city, and they wanted to tell her about what they were going through at school.

When we got married, I realized more what it meant to be married to the oldest sister. I was the only man in the family besides their father, and I was treated like an older brother. When these little sisters couldn't get big sister to do what they wanted, when they wanted her to come home or they wanted to come up to visit, they'd call big brother. It usually worked. They pretty much got their way with me, and she knew it. She understood what they were doing.

Even though they're all grown now and most of them are married, they are still little sisters. Their father is dead, and so I'm treated more like the father. My wife's younger sisters look up to me and respect me enough to call on me for personal matters. I've had to give three away in matrimony and talk to one who wanted my opinion about her upcoming marriage. Sometimes that brings heartache, like when one of her sisters died, but it's never a burden. It's a blessing to be thought of that way.

It's been nice, felt good, to have someone besides my sons from an earlier marriage respecting me and wanting my advice. It's made me feel good because I was the youngest in my family who always had to follow the oldest.

My wife has a great relationship with her family, and that's helped me. They are extremely close even though they're not all in the same city. My family does not have the same closeness. I like the closeness. I like to see them together. Watching all of the sisters around the table trying to talk at the same time is fun and always a time to look forward to.

What would I tell someone who was thinking about marrying an oldest daughter? When you marry an oldest daughter, you're marrying into the head of the family. When anything happens to the mother or father, you become the head of the family. Responsibilities will come to you that you may never have wanted or thought of. Even though you may have a family of your own, you have inherited another family, a complete other family.

I thought of a list of other words one might use in explaining the happiness John describes in his life and marriage. Acceptance. Openness. Willingness to share. Appreciation.

A Love Letter in Disguise

The youngest of three sons, sixty-five-year-old "Gene" is married to an oldest daughter who has three younger siblings. They have been married for forty-two years. Early on, he supported the family. She was a stay-at-home mom until the youngest of their three children reached the age of fourteen.

Over time, he says, their marriage has changed, as he suspects most long-time marriages have. It is now based mostly on individual respect for each other. He says that's "fine," but then he continues.

My wife's position as the oldest daughter has always impacted our marriage because she is happy to take charge if she feels it's important.

Our relationship has changed over the years. When we were first married, it was much more social and equal in terms of what we brought to the table and brought to the marriage. Each of us acted independently and discussed our problems when we saw each other. She had primary responsibility for raising children. I had primary responsibility to support the family. Then our roles changed. As time went on, I became less important in supporting the family and she became more important in terms of wealth.

She's a dynamo—very involved in what's important to her. It all makes me feel like I'm not important to her.

She now travels at least once a month to her hometown where there's a significant family business. That has been a burden on our marriage.

In addition, she has become a pseudo-mother for our pre-school grandchildren. I certainly think it's wonderful for the children and for my daughter. But because my wife is so busy taking care of others, she doesn't have that much time for me. I feel anger and resentment.

These things affect all aspects of our life.

I would like us to become a lot more affectionate, and I would like to spend more time with her in non-business activities. For example, I would like to vacation and travel with her. But her family-business responsibilities cause her to travel, and her trips are never purely recreational.

Although at times we've had fun vacations, I think in general it's hard for her to have fun. I think she feels very responsible for our family and for getting the best for her family.

I understand the responsibilities she has and the difficulties involved in getting the results she wants. I don't know how our daughter would survive without her help. I sometimes think I'm guilty in not helping more. I've turned into a computer nerd, causing me not to be as active in the family as I used to be. A little bit would change if I became more active, but only a little bit. I think she holds on to her responsibilities because she enjoys them so much.

When he had finished baring the emotions he feels as a result of his personal situation, Gene became more detached. He turned his attention toward the implications for marriages in general. "I think it's important for both a wife and her spouse to understand their roles, how they change and then to try to help each other deal with the changes in roles."

If his wife should happen to read this interview, she might not immediately recognize it for what I think it is— a wonderful love letter from a husband who wants to travel with her and experience more affection. This after more than four decades of marriage.

I also thought of the response that many oldest daughters gave to a question in the online survey—*Who was responsible for setting the expectations and standards for you?* Only four percent of oldest daughters chose "self" as the answer. As stressed in the introduction to this chapter, it's hard to see ourselves as we actually are. The view of a spouse can be eye-opening.

True Love

Forty-year-old Michelle grew up with a mother and two grandmothers who were each the first-born females in their respective families. As a result, she saw life modeled in terms of "being responsible for other people and trying to make their lives okay." Not surprising then, as the older sister to a younger brother she found she "knew" very early on what was best for him and what he needed to do.

To further build upon this established family dynamic, when Michelle had been in in her twenties she married a man who was the youngest son in his family of origin. She believes these combined factors contributed to the failure of that first marriage and to "the hardest thing" she has ever done.

I was married to a youngest and because I have a younger brother, we fit like hand in a glove: "Let me tell you how to do it... Let me tell you what you're doing wrong." Then when I was thirty, my marriage fell apart.

I did not really have a clue that my bossiness, my high control, my knowing what was best for another human, my getting in his business and functioning for him were having disastrous effects for both of us. I was living out some of the extremes of being the oldest daughter. And because he was the youngest son, it felt natural for him to have a wife over-function. But until the train wreck happened, I wasn't able to see my part.

There was a defining moment for me when I said, "I don't want to do this to another human being."

That's when I contacted a therapist, a specialist in family systems.[4] *Looking at my part—the fifty percent that I own—was the hardest thing I have ever had to do because it was so ugly. My lack of flexibility. My lack of honoring and respecting differences in another person.*

Through that therapy, I came to understand how being an oldest daughter affects how I live my life, my relationships, my challenges, my strengths. It has helped me observe and moderate some of the polarities of being an oldest. For example, it's difficult for oldests to be vulnerable, to admit we don't have it all together.

I've really tried to manage the extremes of being an oldest because of the devastation some of those characteristics caused in my first marriage. I don't assume anymore I have the right answers for other people. I don't think I know what's best.

I feel the train wreck was the best worst thing that ever happened to me. Before, there was a dogmatic quality about me, a self-righteousness. Now with my important relationships there's a different level of openness, a connectedness I didn't experience before.

Like so many of the personal stories in this book, the one shared above could fit in more than one chapter. "Response-ability" could easily have been home to this story. It's in this chapter because the storyteller talks

---

[4] See Family Systems Therapy in "Resources."

about marriage and how failure can ultimately lead to success.

The saying, "Love means never having to say you're sorry," from the 1970's film *Love Story* has become widely accepted as a truism. I disagree. Saying you're sorry may in fact be the proof of love. We humans make mistakes. Some of them are whoppers. Why not say you're sorry if those mistakes have hurt someone?

Untangling the knots

"Jag," thirty-one, and his wife are parents of two children. At the time of our interview they were expecting a third baby. He describes his wife as the yin to his yang, his opposite. She is "quiet and gentle," whereas he is "good crazy." Jag is the oldest of his parents' four sons. His wife has two younger sisters and one younger brother. Their families had ties with each other before he and his wife met. His younger brother had married one of her younger sisters. But the ties didn't stop there, and knots developed.

Because my brother had married her sister, I knew that my wife was the oldest daughter in her family. But you don't think about it when you like somebody.

Her whole family, not just her siblings, calls my wife. For advice. For info. To complain. To vent out. For some reason, she's the go-to person.

My wife is big-hearted. Sometimes too big-hearted. She hates telling people "no." She goes out of her way to help. It's her nature. She wants to be there for her family. I don't want to change that.

But I don't want her stressing out. She cannot solve their problems. They will not change. Very rarely will they follow her advice. They just want to complain.

When it affects my family, I have to draw the line.

There's a problem now between my wife's sister and her husband. Before now, my wife would have been stressing out about it. But now with her pregnancy, I told her, "You cannot be stressing out over something you have no control over and didn't cause. Your stress can affect our family. Your sisters have too many problems to take on. We have enough of our own."

So my wife told her sister, "Stop calling. Handle your marriage."

I think my wife is burned out. It's been a long time coming. If she stops taking things so much to heart, we'll have a happier, more outgoing wife and mother.

It's made me realize—if I knew someone who might be considering marrying an oldest daughter, I'd tell him, "Know what you're getting into. Know what the family problems are. Believe me, they'll call you, her sisters especially. On some days you won't be the center of attention. Her sisters will be. Be mentally prepared."

Other couples might benefit from the take-charge wisdom of oldest-son Jag and the cooperation of his oldest-daughter wife. Health-care workers are known for telling caregivers, "you can't help someone else unless you first take care of yourself." Much truth to that. Jag and his wife have an increasing number of needs to take care of in their own family, including each other's.

Professional Insight

Love conquers all. Right? Well, hopefully. But a short supply of either time or energy can put even the "truest" love in jeopardy. With the reality today that both are often limited, following three simple steps can help to lessen the stresses that threaten relationships. All three require honest, open communication.

1) Define your marital values and expectations. Identify what both spouses' expectations are and discuss these with each other. It's important for a woman to realize that both partners are responsible for care taking for dependent children and for defining the relationship each wants with the other.

Discussions should include what level of responsibility each has in the marriage as well as in families of origin, which may change as circumstances and life stages change. If an oldest daughter is addressing issues within her family of origin, time may be taken away from the needs of her spouse or children.

2) Identify boundaries. A boundary is where "my responsibility stops and yours starts." All adult children may have to assess their roles with parents and siblings.

A common thread in the spouse stories in this chapter is a willingness on the part of the wife to assist others. Sometimes this is okay with the spouse.

Sometimes it's not. If a spouse has concerns about his wife's choices or her relationships with members of her original family, it is necessary for him to share these concerns. Doing so will allow her to understand how he feels, especially with regard to how this may impact her availability to him and/or their children.

Sharing these concerns directly can avoid resentment from the spouse and lead to a more open and satisfying spousal relationship. However, if one spouse is happy with the status quo and the other wants change, it may be helpful to discuss the differences with a professional marriage therapist.

3) Make changes. If an oldest daughter decides to make changes within her family of origin, I recommend she talk with them directly about these changes. Therefore, when the "rules" or expectations change, everyone is aware. (The exception to this is if in setting different boundaries there is a risk of emotional or physical abuse.) When someone decides to alter behaviors from previous patterns, others may not be accepting of the changes. This may even occur with a spouse who had desired the change, if the altered behavior results in her setting different boundaries with the spouse and asking for more help. Therefore, it is helpful for couples to discuss how the oldest daughter's choices may impact the marriage as well.

Finally, it is best if adults learn to assert their own needs rather than to have others (e.g., spouses) assert for them. That said, it is helpful for spouses to support their wives as they take care of themselves and their families by expressing their boundaries.

For Reflection:

- *What expectations do you have of yourself versus those of your partner in the following areas: childrearing, breadwinner, and housekeeping?*
- *Have you discussed these with your partner?*
- *Have the two of you assumed the roles the other wants?*
- *Have you discussed these directly?*
- Is my wife's availability to her parents/siblings negatively impacting her availability to our family?

Kristin S. Russell, Ph.D.

Old ways die hard
British proverb

Chapter 8.

Across Borders

Oldest Daughter. These two words spoken in numerous languages define a lifetime of experiences for a specific, but countless, population within the human family.

How many oldest daughters are there in the world?

The U.S. Census Bureau can't give even a partial answer. It doesn't add up how many families within our nation have a first-born female child among other siblings. It's understandable. That detail does not affect any policies. To count on getting any such information beyond our borders would be an exercise in fantasy.

I began exploring the story of oldest daughters with a bias. I felt fairly certain that current oldest-daughter responsibilities were probably the result of old-world traditions. I am the third- and fourth-generation daughter of nineteenth-century emigrants from Germany and Ireland. Once in America, they settled on small family farms in communities in Indiana, mid-Missouri and Texas. Therefore, I alternately blamed and credited my rural lineage for the expectations and values with which I'd been brought up. This cultural view was way too near-sighted.

The stories in the following chapter make it abundantly clear. No matter the continent in which a family's roots were laid down, the expectations and responsibilities of oldest daughters are not confined to a particular area. The personal accounts that follow come from regions as disparate as the Middle East and the British Isles as well as from neighboring countries like Mexico.

The feelings first-born females express in their mini-memoirs, including a rarely acknowledged yearning, are nearly indistinguishable from one culture to another. The element of expectations is consistent.

Certain words regularly show up in an oldest daughter's vocabulary no matter her native tongue: responsibility, choice, example and—perhaps the most spirit-rending—if.

The format of this chapter is different. The entire chapter is a compilation of "Other Voices" from around the world. When more than one person from a particular country or region had commented, I selected the account I felt most represented all. Each story provides the perceptions of a first- or second-generation American regarding a family's particular ethnic background and its impact on the life of an oldest daughter in this country.

Though the circumstances, history and locales of these stories vary, a common conundrum emerges. Does the first-born female in a transplanted family stay true to traditions of family and country of origin regardless of the cost to her own hopes? Or if she steps out beyond traditions, does she risk breaking family ties and hearts along the way?

What's an oldest daughter to do?

International Voices with family roots in ...

Africa

What is expected of me is compounded by my being both an African woman and an African Muslim woman. There are certain elements of character, integrity and modesty that I'm supposed to uphold. It's definitely not a choice.

For example, wanting to go to prom is such a simple issue for young American girls. Since I was born here and grew up in (a large Midwestern city), you would think it would be simple for me too. But the idea of a date is nowhere on the agenda for me. And do you have any idea how difficult it is to find a modest prom dress?

My parents struggled with how to be strong parents who upheld their cultural and religious morals while allowing me to live as both a normal American girl and a role model for their other two daughters.

A lot of times I feel like I'm unable to make choices based on myself. I was allowed to do a lot of things, but I set the barre. So I had to think about how what I did would affect my younger sisters. They would always say to our parents, "You let (my name) do this, or wear this..." It was like freedom/restriction.

I'm in graduate school, I have my own responsibilities, and I'm working. Despite all that, I'm not just an older sister. I'm also an additional parent.

My mom uses me as a means to advise my sisters. If there's something she wants to get across to my sisters, she will call and tell me. Then I'm supposed to give my sisters that advice without letting them know I've spoken to her.

When I advise my sisters or talk to them about certain issues, they fully respect me. I appreciate that. However when I'm having a rough day, I don't feel like being a parent. I want to talk to my parent. And sometimes I have to remind my mom of that.

In my house we always had extended family—aunts and grandparents—living with us. Even so, when my parents were away on business trips, I was the one who helped out around house and with the care of my siblings.

My sisters lived completely different lives. It's something being dealt with now. My middle sister is six years younger than me. My baby sister is ten years younger. They have many more privileges than I ever had. It's typical of how older siblings have it. My mom's oldest sister had a more constricted life than her younger sisters.

When my youngest sister was born, I remember my parents saying, "Now you have two younger sisters to think about. They're going to look up to you." At the time

I felt proud. Not to say I don't feel proud now, but then I didn't understand all that was going to entail.

Most of my female friends are oldest siblings with younger sisters, but they are not first generation. We gravitate toward each other. Despite having differing backgrounds, we all share similar stories. The expectations cross cultural and generational lines. We're all like super overachievers.

Anonymous, 25, oldest of three children

I was born and raised in Ethiopia in East Africa but have been in the United States most of my life. My two younger sisters are here, but my oldest is back home. So for the last 25 years, I've been the oldest sister on this end. The responsibility goes from one child to the next. In our tradition that's just the way it is. Looking out for the younger ones is a lifetime commitment for everybody.

But the role of the oldest daughter is different from others in the family. Everybody looks up to her. She really takes on a lot of responsibility and sets the example in respecting elders. Anything her mother or father tell her to do is done, so she's somebody you trust. She is there for you all the time. She is always trying to take up the slack, make you look good. It's a great thing to have someone to look up to, someone to get advice from.

In my culture the oldest daughter's role continues into adulthood. She has the right to choose whether she wants to continue. She can choose not to, but it doesn't happen very often because it's a family thing and a way of life. The family is very close. Whether you've gone away or stay there, the respect and responsibility are there.

Anab, 50, second of four daughters,
functioning as oldest

There's a strong relationship between African-American women and their daughters. It's been there down through the centuries. You can see it in the nurturing and housekeeping role of oldest daughters in Ghana: the oldest daughter helps Mom care for the kids. She's almost a surrogate mother. Mom does laundry and other chores daily. The oldest daughter cares for younger siblings. African girls and African-American girls still carry on the same role: the oldest girl is just expected to be the number-two mother. The oldest male may have assumed some financial responsibility, but he probably did not assume much of the caregiving and the home-support role because that's not the role of men.

Bernard, 55, oldest child/brother of seven siblings,
whose family is from Ghana

Asia

I came to the United States in my early twenties. I started cooking dinner for my whole family at a very young age—seven or eight—and then putting my younger brother to bed. I was like my little brother's little mother. He would follow me all over the place, even to the ladies' bathroom. Now my daughter is like a little mother to my son. She likes to take care of my son.

Traditionally in Chinese culture, the oldest daughter has the most responsibility to take care of the family, no matter what. So she's expected to mature faster, take on more housework, more chores than other siblings. But when it came to sibling fights, she would always be blamed: "You should have known better. You are older." My husband, also raised in China, remembers when he would start a fight, his sister would always be blamed. He's coming to see that it's not quite fair, but he enjoyed it at the time. He enjoyed the privileges. He would always get away with it, but his oldest sister never could.

I accepted the way things were because that was expected, and I never really questioned or doubted. As an adult, I still feel the sense of responsibility. I take care of my husband, family, two children, parents, parents-in-law, and my two brothers. Sometimes it's a little overwhelming. I wish I had time to take care of myself or had someone to take care of me.

I know if I don't take care of—whatever—nobody else will. No matter how tired I am or how bad I feel, I need to do it. I'm tougher and able to handle a lot of situations. I am pretty proud to be the oldest daughter. I feel a responsibility to help everybody. Not just my family. It's part of my nature. I want to offer my talents or knowledge or time to help as many people as possible.

Chinese parents have a tendency to be critical of all children, but especially of the oldest daughter. So oldest daughters tend to be quieter, not as aggressive, afraid of making mistakes. The result of over-criticism.

Helen, 44, one older and one younger brother

I am a second-generation Vietnamese American. Family is a very important part of our culture. I have five younger siblings.

When I was growing up, my friends could go out and stay out late. I didn't have that opportunity because as the oldest daughter, I was expected to come home and help around the house. If I'd been born a male, the expectations would have been different. Males in my culture have more freedom than females.

Other things were expected of me very early that weren't expected of my siblings. When they were all little, I was responsible for quieting them, giving them bottles and baths, changing their diapers. During summers, Dad would have a list for me, like doing laundry and fixing lunch. I would need to have it completed before he came home. Sometimes I considered myself a servant.

When my sister and brothers were teenagers, I was responsible for teaching them. If they didn't do good on a test, my parents asked me, 'Why didn't you teach them better? Or teach them to fold the clothes correctly?'

Who helped me? No one really. Mostly just me.

My parents want me to put family over everything else. They realize school is important, but they want me to do that on my own time.

My curfew, even now when I am in college, is 10 p.m. So I plan out everything, when I'm going to leave, when I'm going to arrive, how long it takes me to walk from one location—I feel this makes me more responsible because I need to be home early to help take care of my siblings and help out my parents.

I'm lucky to be part of a (religious/ethnic) organization on campus. My mother was part of the same group when she was in college. There are about forty members, including other oldest daughters, but none who still live with their families or have big families. Usually they're the oldest of two. They're not regarded in the same way. Our group looks on me as a mother figure. I'm always there when they need to talk. When they're having problems in some area of their life, I help them balance things. I like whenever they need help. I think of it as having fun by helping others.

We go camping every year and give each other nicknames that describe our personalities. Mine is "Mother Cat." I understand, but there are times I wish I didn't have to be the mother. I guess I don't like always being in a mother role and would like to have more fun.

I feel the need to be useful and to be appreciated. I worry about getting burned out, but I find a lot of satisfaction in helping others. This is my line of reasoning—we need other things in life to help keep us balanced. Even though my parents want me to spend 100% on my family, having school and friends and being of service to all of them helps diversify me. Helping others besides my family is like taking a little vacation.

Vietnamese have a very strong sense of family. We are expected to take care of our parents. I do not feel I have a choice. Sometimes it's frustrating, but I try to look at the good side of it. My brothers and my sister and I have really good times together.

Mary, 21, oldest of five

Great Britain

I didn't like being the oldest. I always had to take responsibility. It was drilled into me that I set the example. I had the role of a mother when my mother was working, particularly during long school vacations when I was expected to be in charge. I never went to someone else's house and hung out. I sound like Cinderella, but I never thought of myself that way. My experience as oldest made me very determined to go to college. And I did, even though in England (then) only twenty-five percent went on to college. It was very select.

I realized how much I'd been robbed of my own childhood by discovering Legos when I was thirty-one years old and playing with my own four-year-old. I understood then that I hadn't played as a child.

It took a long time for my brothers and sisters to see me as a sister, not as a surrogate parent. I do know I'm absolutely vital to the whole family setup. Just a couple of days ago—and mind you, I'm a continent away in America now—my brother called to tell me of a success. Another brother called recently to tell me "I've done it," before he told his wife. He just knew that I knew what it had taken to get there!

Ann, 48, oldest of eight children

Eastern Europe

My great-grandmother was born and raised in what was then Yugoslavia, now Croatia. She didn't really talk about the old country, but she said to me, "It's a big responsibility being the oldest." She was the oldest of three. My grandmother was the oldest of nine. She lived in Alaska. I was very close to my grandmother. We would talk about being the oldest daughter. I remember her telling me that her two older brothers weren't expected to help at home because they were already out on a fishing boat with their father. She went to work in the cannery at age thirteen. But then when she got home, she was required to keep things going there. I remember her saying, "Things are different for girls."

We would be talking in the kitchen and she'd put a stool in front of the stove. She taught me how to cook, how to brown hamburger. When I was four years old, I was making spaghetti sauce. I could bake. I ironed. I laughed to myself the other day when I was ironing—like my grandmother taught me! Her attitude was I was the oldest, and she was going to teach me how to do things so I could do them early and well.

My mom was sickly, so my grandmother taught me basically how to step up and be the mother. My mother expected that, too. It was very clear, very early on. Somebody had to keep the house going and that fell to me. When I was nine or ten I was babysitting. By the time I was eleven, I was taking care of a household of kids and animals. The attitude was always, "You're the oldest. Set the example."

I resented it especially when I got into high school and realized my peer group didn't have the same expectations. I don't remember having a childhood, of relaxing. Instead I remember crushing responsibilities. I never have been able to establish a sibling relationship with my younger siblings because I was viewed as a substitute mother.

The message was communicated very early on, "You're the role model. You have to do (whatever)."

I still have an overwhelming sense of responsibility. It doesn't frighten me. I have always risen to be a leader. So it's a good thing, I guess, that along the way I developed a good measure of self-confidence.

But if I'd been a male, I wouldn't have been making spaghetti for an entire family at age five.

Tia, 50, oldest of eight

The Middle East

My father is Lebanese. When I was in kindergarten, he told me, "You are a (family surname) and you will do nothing to tarnish the name." I inherently knew I should be the example. I hated it. I always felt like an adult. I never got to have the fun. It was hard. I always felt like I had to walk the straight and narrow. My brothers and sister were more carefree.

I think oldest daughters inherently know they're being looked up to. My brother, as the oldest son, didn't feel that way. He could get away with things. I was expected to be respectful of my parents, to agree with our father as the head of the family, and to learn and carry on traditions.

What's interesting in an ethnic family is that a father generally would like the eldest to be a son. I worked incredibly hard to be an equal to my brothers in my father's eyes, but I knew it was never going to happen. I do believe I crossed that "equal" threshold when I finally became established in my career and was able to open some doors for myself. I got involved in an industry my dad had always wanted to be a part of. He respected that.

Pulling the family together is the only thing I know how to do. As far as keeping the family together, I like doing that. Thinking of myself as an oldest daughter will never go away.

"Gina," 50, oldest of four

The Pacific Islands

When it comes to responsibility, I'm it. As I get older, it seems there's a difference between me and my younger sister and my two brothers. They continue to live in the Philippines. I am now in the United States. I have more responsibility for the financial care of my parents. Maybe we're brought up that way. I have a feeling that if the first one in my family were my brother, it would have fallen on him. I don't think it's gender. I think it's being the oldest. In our culture, the first child is expected to be responsible—as an adult! This responsibility is not placed on children.

"Luchi," 68, oldest of four

North America

I'm second-generation Mexican-American, the oldest child and only girl. My father placed a lot of responsibility on me. I was to take care of the whole household and do all the things that my mother would do plus raise my three brothers when my mother was working. My brothers had time to play. I didn't.

My dad kept tabs on me night and day. He didn't do that with my brothers because they were boys. He knew he was treating us differently. I was the girl. He wanted to make sure that nothing would happen to me or shame the family name. My father was very proud of his name. He made sure I was watched almost twenty-four hours.

To this day, he relies on me to do things like setting up my parents' cell phone, programming their computers, re-doing an outdoor kitchen. My brothers could do these, but I don't know if he even asks them. I guess I've learned to accept this. It's been the role I've had all my life.

In the Hispanic culture, family is very important—and the oldest daughter does take care of a lot of things. If I stopped handling responsibility for my family, I don't know what I would do. It would feel like I wasn't doing my job. I would feel confused because I have done this all of my life. Making my mom and dad happy is very important to me.

Ramona, 51, three younger brothers

My dad is Native American, my mom is white. I was two years old when my biological dad left, but my mother kept us involved in the community.

I didn't have a full childhood. It probably stopped the summer vacation of my seventh-grade year. Mom worked, and that was the year she decided we didn't have to go to the baby sitter, that we could save money if I watched my younger siblings.

I remember feeling overwhelmed. I had to get all the laundry out to dry, bring it back in, do the cooking all day while my little sisters and brother got to play and watch TV. After school started again, I had to make sure they did their homework and got their baths. I think it's probably just how it's supposed to be. My mom was a single mother. She needed help from somebody else.

My ethnicity played a role in that. The Native American community has very strong ties with family. I felt that was my role, to do the mothering when my mother couldn't do it. The responsibility for my younger siblings just fell on my shoulders as the next oldest person in the family.

I'm probably still very mothering to my siblings, even though they're all adults now and probably don't want to hear stuff from me. When my sisters or brother need something or are in trouble, I feel like it's my place to be there for them. I still feel like I don't have any choices about this.

I don't know who's there for me. I've never really thought about it. They are to an extent, but not to the same extent.

Rhoda, 25, oldest of four children

The oldest daughter is a pivotal role in the family. My role was to take care of the family well. That meant for me, as a West Indian and American, there were very high expectations placed on me by my mother, my father, my elders in Barbados—"You will carry on in the family, do more than what we (parents) have done." It was an expectation that our parents had, to make them proud. Being the oldest child, I was the one on whom they placed the first expectations. If my sister had been born first, she would have it. But she had such a bright, easy time. My younger sister had so much fun growing up. She was the adventurous one. She wasn't structured.

I had a doctrine of regimentation, order. I was expected to go to school, then come and give back to the people of the island. My upbringing clearly prepared me. My family set the expectations and provided the opportunity that enabled me to flourish.

I was the one who had tea with my grandmother. I learned to have tea in the silence of that room, how to live within that room and within myself. When I was older, I still went to my grandmother's. My sister didn't have to. It wasn't important for her. It was important for me because I was the oldest. My grandmother was one of the cornerstones to my foundation for my future. I learned how to do things the right way. She taught me "process" without that word. But in addition, what I learned, would be a meditative experience.

It gave me the structure to do what I have done in my international business career—the adventures, travels to England, Paris... It just happened when I went off to (a job) in Europe. My sister said,"How???" But I just did it. I had a job to do and just did it.

I realize there was a difference in expectations for the two of us. The expectations were the same that both of us would be successful. My family's hopes, based on what I demonstrated were higher. I was the oldest.

Thaïs, 58, one younger sister

"What takes real courage is choosing to live, choosing to save herself at all costs.
The White Mary, Kira Salak

Chapter 9.

Change, please

A few years ago I attended a women's luncheon at which a three-term office-holder—a spunky, sparkling, red-haired Irish woman—was the guest speaker. After her talk a member of the audience asked her a fairly routine question. "What motivated you to go into public service?" The answer was neither routine nor expected.

She began by saying that she was the first-born of several children in her family, a position that encouraged leadership. Then the popular official laughingly added, "And if I come back in another life, it won't be as the oldest daughter!" While still in this life, however, she said she was putting her extended family on notice that she would no longer be fixing the holiday dinners. The audience responded to her comments with chuckles and even a few cheers.

What caused this politically astute woman to make those remarks about being an oldest daughter? What made audience members react as they did? On whose behalf did the listeners hope to see the changes made? Was this really about holiday dinners? Or was there something else going on?

I asked a first-born female from one family and a younger sister from a different family for their takes on the incident. The oldest daughter immediately replied, "You mean like the expectation that, *of course*, we'll have the dinner"?

The younger sibling had more to say. "Oldest daughters seem to always have the dinner and then complain about it. Like one I know who says she feels like she's being 'used.' I asked why she didn't suggest that someone else host the dinner for a change. But, 'oh, no,' she can't relinquish it. How is it helping anybody if you're feeling resentful?"

I felt compelled to ask this younger daughter a follow-up question. What if nobody steps up and offers to have the dinner? She shrugged, "Then you say, I guess we won't have a family dinner for everybody this year." As noted earlier, response-ability.

I caught an uncomfortable glimpse of myself in the mirror of her comments. Why did things have to be the way they'd always been? Though one of my sisters once hosted a beautiful, traditional Thanksgiving dinner for our family, the majority of the holiday meals were held at my encouragement at my house.

I had always felt it was my responsibility to bring everyone together as my mother had done. So I continued doing so, even as our extended family increased, the scheduling conflicts multiplied, and my energy became more limited.

After several months of discussions with my sisters, we mutually decided one year to have a "come when you can" get-together around Thanksgiving desserts instead of before a dressed turkey. China and silver optional. We put into practice an important realization. What's important is not where the dining room table is located or what's on it, but whose feet are under it. That new tradition continues.

Now here comes the disturbing part of my story. I actually said to my husband, "I hope Mom wouldn't have been disappointed by these changes." Do you know how old I was when I said that to him?! (I'm not revealing.) It slowly registered that there'd been a word scrawled on the fogged mirror of that younger daughter's earlier comments. *Expectations.* Mine. Possibly leftover from childhood. But as an adult, I owned them.

The stories in this chapter describe the struggles and decisions of real-life oldest daughters and siblings alike.

Facing expectations set for or held by them. Deciding if and when changes are called for.

Breaking Point

Change began for "Trudy" with a shattering experience. It occurred when she was a teenager, alone in her family's living room.

She recalled the moment decades later as a fifty-five-year-old woman. She now divides her time between responsibilities as a respected professional and commitments as a married mother of three. But back then, things were different. The oldest of eight children was a "compliant" child who went along with the rules and did what was expected of her. Up to a point.

When I was four years old, my mother also had a three-year-old, a two-year-old, a one-year-old, was soon to be pregnant again—and no help. For years, my mother said she couldn't have done it if she hadn't had me. I got much reinforcement for being a good little girl and Mommy's Little Helper, doing what I was told to do and being happy.

When I think about myself then, I see a little girl with pigtails who is really young, very responsible, able to take care of things. When she's at home, this little girl is in complete control, bossing her brothers and sisters. But when she's in her social sphere with others her age, she is pretty shy and quiet because she doesn't get to play very much.

I was confused by my role. Sometimes I felt really honored because I got so many kudos at home. But as I got older, I began to experience resentment. For example, our parents had told us if we wanted private schooling for high school, we'd have to pay for it. I did. But my brother who was a few years younger did not have to help pay for his private schooling. When I found this out, I was a junior or senior in high school. I was very angry.

So one day I walked over to a liqueur set that was special to my mother. I took all of the little glasses and stacked them up on top of each other and then I kind of pinged them with my finger, and they all tumbled down and broke. I just went, "Oh, well." And it felt so good. Looking back at what was pretty risky behavior for me, I realize this was my way of acting out my anger—maybe for the first time.

In the summers between my college years, I had a chance to do some traveling outside my home state. That's when the world totally opened up. After I came back from one of those trips, I informed my family I was moving out of our house. I knew that my parents would be devastated, but wasn't prepared for how upset my brothers and sisters were. I told them, "Believe me—you will thank me one day." And they have. Then when I was twenty-one and moved completely out of the city, they didn't like that either. But I'm like, "You've gotta be kidding me. There are so many exciting things to do in the world."

I had a lot of responsibilities when I was growing up. But when I left, I really left. The town and all the expectations. It was a very conscious decision to move away. No second thoughts. No guilt. I just intuitively knew it was the right thing to do.

I've been very blessed in everything I've done since. Things have just fallen into my lap, mostly in the field of human services.

I'm very different from the rest of my family. I'm definitely not compliant. I push boundaries a lot in a respectful way. I still consider myself the oldest daughter. But I don't believe oldest daughters should continue to fill family expectations after everyone's grown. I haven't. I don't think it was a formal, conscious decision. It happened naturally when I moved out.

I'm not the matriarch of the family. I don't have that role. I'm just not into the power thing.

We all know the feeling of having reached a breaking point. Trudy reached it as a teenager. Her mother's prized glasses literally took the hit.

Resentment isn't pretty. Neither is unfairness. Before either could take a toll on her future life, Trudy left them behind.

Essential to her success in moving away from her family is the "why" that led to it. It wasn't the anger that showed in the reflexive swipe she took at the hapless crystal set. Nor was it a knee-jerk decision. Awareness, observation, and thoughtful consideration led to her departure. Even if the unknown lay ahead, the benefits reasonably outweighed the risks. She intuitively knew it was the right thing to do.

Trudy still thinks of herself as the oldest daughter. That's part of who she is. What she didn't take with her or accept for herself were the expectations others had for her because of her position by birth in the family.

Distancing

Jody's position in her family puts her smack dab in the middle. The now forty-year-old was born three years after her older sister and three years before her younger sister.

Family expectations had always been the same for each of the three siblings. Make good grades, come home on time, and set a good example. Jody chuckles, remembering that the oldest daughter in her family "didn't do any of that." She ran away from the prescribed model from the get-go.

My oldest sister really wouldn't follow anybody's rules, not even those of my parents. She was always staying out late, always breaking curfews, always grounded.

A lot of times I just stood there, cocked my head and wondered—"What the hell is she thinking?" I felt kind of bad for her. It wasn't as if the rules were any surprise in our household. Everybody knew what they were.

She set the example for what I wasn't to do. I watched her and learned to calculate my risks, to mitigate them on all fronts and then decide if it was worth it.

She married when she was twenty and remained married for approximately ten years. During that time our parents divorced, and she had expectations of herself on two fronts. Early on in that ten years, she was very intense, focused on trying to ensure that things would happen the way they should. Probably for most of her marriage, she became the one who got everyone together at her house and tried to juggle between Mom and Dad. Typical oldest-daughter response.

We've talked about that a lot. She felt she had the duty to provide a sense of family, even though we didn't feel like much of a family for a while. She tried to become the peacemaker and fixer. Nobody expected that of her. She expected it of herself.

After her own divorce, she moved to Europe. In some ways I then assumed the familial responsibility. She had the sense to tell me, "This is not your responsibility, not your job. Stop already. I've been through this. It's not your job to ensure that people do what they're 'supposed' to do—whatever that may be."

Jody could be the model for oldest-daughter watchers. She observed, evaluated and learned what not to do from watching her oldest sister and then later on from listening to her. A sort of worst-practices but best-advice scenario.

Not to be overlooked in Jody's decades-long, clear-eyed observations is a comment she makes about the tumult that ensued following their parents' divorce. Jody points out that no one forced or expected the oldest of the three daughters to take on salvaging the family. She did it herself. It's part of what is often described as the oldest-daughter syndrome. First-born females commonly expect themselves to be responsible for fixing things, especially where younger siblings are concerned.

When Jody became the "functional" oldest daughter after her sister literally left the country, Jody could have taken on the tendency to fix. That she didn't is a credit to her sister's wise advice and her own willingness to continue learning what not to do.

"Why Tell a Story" Story

In writing this book, I deliberately omitted any stories of abuse that I heard in interviews. Abuse is such a complex, difficult topic that I didn't want to discuss it as a non-expert. I also had no idea how common oldest-daughter abuse is. I'd never seen and still haven't seen a study on abuse in that specific category.

However, I don't want to have it said that I played it safe in writing this book. I acknowledge that heart-, body- and spirit-breaking things happen to innocent people. The following story acknowledges that reality. And goes beyond it.

I met forty-five-year-old Jan when we were both appearing on a local radio program. I was there as the author of an upcoming book. She was there as the executive director of a nonprofit organization. After learning my book was about oldest daughters, she offered to meet me later and tell me her own story.

Our interview took place at this busy woman's home. Busy is an understatement. In addition to her professional position, she is also a single mother of six. That afternoon she was getting ready to go camping with her children and at the same time making a prom dress for her oldest daughter. These light-hearted activities contrasted dramatically with the narrative Jan would tell of her childhood and teenage years in a "very abusive home."

As the oldest of five children, she felt from a young age that she was responsible for protecting her siblings. That mostly meant deflecting the blows from their abusive father. Then at age seventeen, she gave up and moved physically away from home. However, the proverbial "you take yourself wherever you go" followed Jan.

Absolutely one could say I'm still trying to take care of the world. Even though I left home, I continue to have that sense of responsibility. I just transferred it and manifested it as caretaking—marrying three husbands who needed it, having six children of my own, and then working in the nonprofit world.

Over time, I decided to change. It took years of hard work looking at my life. I remember asking in therapy, "If I quit being a workaholic, what will I be?" I was continually trying to prove that I had worth by helping others.

I've learned there's a difference between responsibility and caretaking. Caretaking, as I see it, has a lot to do with controlling other people—not being able to separate one's own expectations from letting people have their own lives.

People want to be taken care of, and I have had a hard time catching that before getting sucked into it. When people call and ask, "What shall I do about xx?" I can either caretake and tell them what to do, or I can give them info about where they can get help to be responsible for themselves. When they ask, "What should I believe, what should I think?" I have learned not to answer for them. I can give them resources, but then they have to research and come to their own conclusions about what they believe.

It took about ten years to make the changes stick for me. A lot of that time was spent on my own—reflecting, writing, regressing, progressing. So, I don't know if it takes therapy for everyone, but most of us just don't become aware that we have choices.

There comes a time when it's okay to have your own life. It's usually pretty hard work to change old patterns, but it's well worth it.

Jan is no longer close to her family of origin. "Opting out," as she puts it, did not end the sense of responsibility for others that she grew up with. But the changes that she has made with much effort have allowed her over time to live her life very differently.

Jan's story appears in this chapter because of the messages I believe are in it for those who might be wondering if their lives could benefit from making changes that require courage and effort.

Disrupting a Dynasty

It was a cheating scoundrel who ultimately brought changes to a four-generation dynasty of oldest daughters.

Forty-three-year-old Wynne is a married mother of two who grew up in the shade of a formidable family tree. She is the oldest daughter of an oldest daughter of an only daughter of an oldest daughter. Remarkably, she knew each of them.

Wynne was eleven years old when her great-grandmother died. Old enough to have formed a distinct impression that the first of the family's oldest-daughter progenitors was someone who "would do anything for us."

Next in line, Wynne's grandmother. A woman who "did it all." She married at sixteen and raised two daughters while caring for her own ailing grandmother. If this weren't enough, at the same time she operated a beauty shop out of the back of her home. In keeping with her times, she also followed the decisions made by her husband.

None of this family modeling would have been lost on Wynne's mother. She became a wife and a married mother of three with a part-time career. She is a woman Wynne describes as "very self-sacrificing at her core."

Wynne, the oldest of her three siblings might have become a fourth-generation version of these women. But a devastating personal situation caused her to question herself, to talk to a family therapist and eventually to break the dynastic mold.

I had broken up with a man I'd been dating for two years after I learned he'd been cheating on me. I began to ask myself, "Where am I headed? What's going to happen to me? Why am I the way I am, so intense, always the problem solver?"

To find the answers, I sought help through the Employee Assistance Program where I worked. I was put in touch with a family-systems therapist. [5]

With her help, I came to look in a much broader way at how families work. I began to understand the generational picture and how it has affected me.

In general, there's a lot of pressure to try to have things how they've always been. I see my mother doing what she saw my grandmother and great-grandmother do, to be child- and others-focused. What she and her mother and her grandmother did could also be indicative of an oldest daughter's belief that "nobody else can do it as well."

I am prone to that feeling, too. It's the typical oldest's belief that you know how to do it best.

But there's a significant difference between me and the expectations of previous generations just to do what had been done before. In my generation, we have the opportunity to see choices. People are doing more work on themselves. So when a person realizes "these things are not working so well for me" and understands the long-term impact of staying the course, we can see the benefits of changing, stirring the pot...

That's especially difficult when your mom is an oldest. You want her to think you're doing a good job. For a very long time I would get defensive. I felt I had let

---

[5] See Resources: Family Systems Therapy

my mom down because I wasn't living up to her standards, doing too many things that are not just focused on my children, being too involved in other things that are important just to me. That's not a criticism of my mom. That was a learning experience for me. It caused arguments between us because I was being defensive about doing things differently.

Eventually I explained to her that she had had expectations for me about college. That I, along with my siblings, could do just about anything we wanted. I don't think she had that expectation for herself. She's seen the change in me. She is supportive of the work I've done and appreciates that I'm open to what she has to say. She's sometimes right, too.

I have in common with my mom, my grandmother and my great-grandmother the learned behavior and expectation that oldest daughters are expected to focus on other family members, not on themselves. But I am able to say that there are things I'm going to do that take care of myself.

"I can only change myself and sometimes that changes everything." I have that quote on my refrigerator.

Wynne had an unusual personal laboratory in which to learn about and from first-born females. She was able to observe characteristics and family expectations up close and personally. She appears early on to have accepted and even admired the way her mother, grandmother, and great-grandmother put everyone else first. But circumstances and therapy led to changes in that pattern of thinking.

This child of the late twentieth century had been brought up to think she could accomplish whatever she wanted. That's a distinct disconnect from being conditioned to do only what's expected, as was the case with her predecessors.

According to the experts, change occurs when a person is uncomfortable enough to allow it to happen. Then it actually takes place if and when a person has the courage to take whatever steps are necessary.

Kudos to Wynne for questioning herself and seeking help. While acknowledging her heritage with respect, she ultimately determined that she had the right to change the way things had been done in order to personally benefit as an individual within the family.

Professional Insight

In prior chapters, I've discussed the importance of adults evaluating for themselves the roles they want to play. So true in this chapter!

In general, it's been my observation that oldest daughters tend to be very responsible, to be very successful in the workplace, and to share a tendency to not allow themselves to have as much fun as their siblings.

Just as it is unfair and unhealthy to have children take on parental roles (when a parent is capable of doing so), it is also not in a child's best interest for parents to project unfulfilled dreams onto their kids.

If you were raised to do so, it is important as an adult to decide if this is the role you want for yourself. If not, I encourage you to give yourself permission to function in the role you want in your family (e.g., to be a peer sibling, not a parent). Setting limits for yourself may result in the need for others to pick up what you have been doing or to show a willingness to help.

Your parents, and possibly others, too, may be disappointed or angry with your choices. If this happens and is hard for you to cope, it may be helpful to find a professional to talk with who can assist you in learning how to listen to your own voice.

Whatever your decisions, it's probably helpful to realize it takes time for both you and other members of your family to become adjusted to any changes you choose to make.

For Reflection:

- *Have you spent some time alone with yourself to figure out who YOU want to be? Have you given enough time to thinking about what's important for YOU to do*
- *Are you willing to give up the kudos that go along with being the perennial family host or the admiration that may come with being the person others always come to for advice?*
- *Have you let others know that you would appreciate and welcome their help?*
- *Before you make any decisions that would significantly alter your relationship with a member of your family, have you talked about possible alternate solutions? Sometimes it is best to get these opinions from other family members, sometimes from friends outside the family.*

Kristin S. Russell, Ph.D.

I'm Nobody! Who are you?
Are you—Nobody—too?
"I'm Nobody! Who are you?" by Emily Dickinson

Chapter 10.

Selfies

"What do you want to be when you grow up?"

It's an age-old question. And, at least in recent times, an ageless one. Asked of five-year-olds, sixty-five-year-olds, those in between and beyond. It can be a thought-provoking and even exciting query. What do you envision for yourself in the future?

For your SELF.

Self is a funny word. It rarely occurs as a stand-alone. It's almost always used with another. Self-assured. Self-centered. Selfless. Self-reliant. Self-sufficient. Myself. Yourself. Herself.

Unless you take the stand-alone word that's everywhere these days. *Selfie*. The snapshot of a person, taken in a memorable place or with a memorable person. Not intended to be a true picture of who the selfie really is, just a glimpse of a life.

So, back to basics. What does "self" mean?

Defining her "self," apart from her position in the family, is a task that often seems particularly challenging for an oldest daughter. It sometimes keeps her from answering, or even asking, who she wants to be well into her grown-up years.

The previous nine chapters have examined the "selves" of oldest daughters in their relationship to siblings and spouses. Sometimes these first-born females have come across as heroines, other times as villains. Sometimes even as the victims of circumstances.

The first two narratives in this chapter describe what happens when an oldest daughter or family member takes stock of what lies ahead for her as she continues to grow.

The last story, "Book End," is mine. It follows the final "Professional Insight."

The Achievement Syndrome

You may remember meeting Jennifer in Chapter 2. She was the small child who suddenly became aware of her ability to lead those around her. In that chapter she explained how, even though she was technically the third-born child in the family, circumstances had left her functioning as the oldest child. She accepted her position in the family and what came along with it, including her position as "first in line," leader and achiever.

Then, at age fifty-two, and successful by all the usual corporate standards of money and title, Jennifer began to question and re-evaluate what she'd always accepted in terms of her own expectations.

Most of my life I have wanted to achieve what I thought was the right thing, based on what my family, parents, society wanted in a general sense. Now that I'm older, I still want to continue to lead and achieve, but I have a different sense of achievement.

I still have a sense of responsibility. But in the past I thought achievement meant making money and achieving a position, receiving some sort of status. Achievement had to be tangible, have a title. I felt good about my successes.

Now I'm focusing more on the community level than on my professional life. My sense now is that money and title aren't that important. I'm more interested in doing something for the public good, for the neighborhood or region, in helping organize local events.

I have shifted from being a professional achiever to a community giver. The reward is very different. The satisfaction of working with people on a community level is amazing. It's very different from when I was growing up, and from when I was a professional achiever and associated achievement with money and position.

My expectations of myself have changed as an adult.

"Success" is a word I heard often as I talked with or interviewed oldest daughters. Sometimes the term was spoken proudly, other times wistfully, depending on how the person saw her life. I'm not sure if achievement and success are commonly interchangeable, but I have the feeling that Jennifer would describe what she is now achieving as "success."

Boundary Hunting

Expectations and images from two decades ago have stayed with "Cece" into adulthood. She has vivid memories of herself standing in her family's kitchen with its green refrigerator and gas stove. Command Central. From there, her parents expected her to run the household, make sure her younger brother and sister were taken care of, and have dinner on the table at the end of the day.

In her mind's eye, she sees the teenage Cece watching from the kitchen window as her six-year-old brother and ten-year-old sister play kickball and tag in the yard. Not her life. Her own connection with the outside world and her friends was through a long, curly cord that stretched the length of the kitchen from a yellow telephone to a hall around the corner.

It would be more than a decade before she moved the center of control from her family to herself. During studies as a thirty-something seminary student, she allowed serious self-reflection to lead her to personal counseling and a decision "to go through some things head on" in order to have a future for herself. I interviewed her twice. In the first one, she explained:

I've been trying to find out who I am, why I behave and react the way I do, and why I care so much. I'm thirty-four years old and still trying to figure things out because I basically didn't get the guidance I've needed—even while I was providing guidance to my sisters and brothers and, it seems like, everybody else in the world.

I have loving, supportive parents. They did the best they knew how to do. But as the product of teenage parents, I grew up along with my mom and dad. That's not a good thing. By the time my sister and brother came along, everything was in place for them.

Being the oldest child in my experience has been such a struggle. It robbed me of my childhood. I didn't realize that at the time. I thought I was just being responsible or more mature than my peers. Being the oldest and a daughter is a double burden. You're expected to do everything the wife and mother does or does not do. Plus my ethnicity places more responsibility on women.

Now as a black woman who is also a first-generation (to be) out of housing projects, I feel fortunate, blessed and obligated to help everyone else. My heart is heavy from it, and I'm tired. I feel like I have been taken for granted.

The only time I have ever felt validated, loved, or comforted is when I have been doing for others. Assisting others even transferred into my professional life. Most of my life (hmph), until now, I have been an administrative "assistant," even though I basically ran my department.

It's dawned on me that I have to begin to search for and live my dreams.

Once I came to that realization, I could begin making the decisions I needed for me, for Cece. I began by relating to my family in a different way. I no longer call home every day. If it's convenient for me, I will take their calls. They notice the changes, but they think it's because I'm dating. They tried to make that as an excuse. I'm not letting them do that.

Three years later, Cece, now a professional counselor, agreed to a follow-up interview regarding those personal resolutions she had made.

I have changed my life the way I intended to. It has been a great relief. I have created boundaries. I'm no longer a people-pleaser. I've learned it's okay to say, 'no.'

As for my family's reaction to the changes I've made—my mother has been supportive. I don't think my father understood. My sister and brother—I don't think they even really noticed. They are just concerned about their worlds and that's the way it's always been. I think that's because they're younger siblings and they never had the responsibility I had as the oldest sister.

I'm no longer that sister. I began to take care of myself, to love myself more, to spend time with myself, to do the things that bring happiness and pleasure to Cece.

I'm okay with the title of oldest daughter. It requires me to be different. I'm the change agent.

"Who I am as an individual" vs. "Who I am as the oldest daughter" is a question that confronts many first-born daughters in adulthood. Cece had two advantages and used them: taking time to reflect on what's important to herself apart from her family, and investing in personal counseling. Both helped her decide to leave behind old expectations. Then she actually stuck to the boundaries she created and became a change agent for herself.

Professional Insight

This final chapter asks you to consider, "Are you living the life you want for yourself?" or "Are you living your life the way others want or expect of you?"

Previous "Insights" have explored issues critical to understanding this question and the way you choose to answer it. They have also encouraged you to explore your authentic self.

If you have recognized that you'd like to make changes, doing that can be easier said than done. As we've previously pointed out and some of the stories and comments have shown, not everyone will be happy if you choose to start making changes for yourself. Especially if this means you're no longer meeting others' needs in the way they want.

Change may make both you and others uncomfortable. To do what you need for yourself when others do not agree can be anxiety provoking. As previously discussed, it is helpful to learn skills to tolerate this anxiety, whether through self-help books, therapy, or discussions with others who support you. I encourage you to choose the type of support that is best for you.

For Reflection:

- *What type of support do I need if I am thinking about making changes for myself? A support group of friends? Other supportive family-of-origin members? My spouse or partner? A professional therapist?*
- *What, if anything, will I risk if I make changes in the way I live my life?*
- *If I do not make changes, can I be happy with the way I'm living my life now?*

Kristin S. Russell, Ph.D.

Patricia Schudy

Book End

Rob and I were sitting at a round table in front of and just slightly below the speaker's podium at a local literary fundraiser. The guest of honor, a well-known New York author, had just published a non-fiction book about a famous artist. He looked out over our heads at the attentive crowd. "My wife and I are pleased to be here for a number of reasons," he began. "Not the least of which is that the publication of this book marks the end of ten years of concentrated effort!"

I glanced over at my husband and saw the deer-in-the-headlights look in his eyes. *Ten years*?

I had just begun gathering information for a possible book about oldest daughters. The idea that it would/could possibly take ten years out of our lives was unthinkable. Surely not. But yes.

Doing research, creating an online survey and monitoring the results. Developing a database. Interviewing more individuals in various birth-order positions and relationships than I could possibly include. These required hours, days, weeks, months. It was only the beginning.

What could not be rushed or deadlined was mining the meaning from the notebooks full of information I'd gathered. Translating into words that both minds and hearts could understand would take time and required that I learn a new writing language.

It took a couple of years and innumerable trashed efforts for me to come down from my lofty safe place as the observing journalist I'd always been and reluctantly become a participant in my own story. I had to learn to sweep aside pride and privacy, to open my heart and reveal my personal self—proverbial warts and all. I had to tell the meaning I found in my personal story if I expected others' stories to have meaning.

It wasn't all somber work. There is humor in the twists and turns of even serious "facts." Take the following ironies—

- A fifty-one-year-old oldest daughter who identifies her adult occupation as "Compliance Officer." I don't know if she had to list experience with younger siblings as part of her credentials.
- The third of three daughters who says she learned to mitigate her losses by watching her oldest sister and avoiding things that got her into trouble. This youngest's adult occupation—investment counselor.
- The oldest daughter who says she is "trying to get out of the habit of telling people what to do." She is the successful author of self-help books.

I'm not making any of this up.

Early on I had had a mostly unstated hope that *Oldest Daughters: What to Know...* would help readers understand what it's like to be born into that position and have its responsibilities continue for a lifetime. Now I know that Responsibilities get a bum rap. The culprit is really Expectations. The ones that come along with the job title (a job we didn't apply for, let it be noted) of oldest daughter. And the ones we set for ourselves.

I was especially, silently hoping my family would gain more empathy for what I felt had been expected of me. But somewhere along the interview road that I walked to write this book, one shoe slipped onto the other foot. I came to understand what it's like to have an oldest daughter as a sibling or spouse. I discovered that resentment and appreciation exist on both sides of the sibling fence regarding the expectations placed on oldest daughters by her parents and subsequently continued by her siblings or herself.

It's a cliché that writers don't necessarily change things or others, but writing changes the writers. I learned to see myself through the eyes of those closest to me. As the poet Robert Frost noted, "And that has made all the difference." Certainly that's true in the clarification of misunderstandings, the healing of old wounds, and the closer relationships I now enjoy.

As I wrote I recognized the kindred spirit I share with other oldest daughters. I acknowledge that the stories I have shared in this book are ones that spoke to me as I interviewed. They may unintentionally reflect some of my own feelings.

I have become keenly sensitive to the value of family relationships and what goes into making or breaking them. I remain convinced that—

- Being born the first child, the oldest daughter, of my parents describes my place in my family of origin. It does not define who I am.
- As adults, oldest daughters have no more or different obligations to younger siblings (absent disabling circumstances) than all siblings have to one another.
- An oldest daughter's childhood responsibilities and expectations can continue to affect her relationships throughout adulthood.

For these reasons, I wrote this book.

I hope that, as readers, you have found yourself becoming more aware of the way oldest daughters, siblings and/or spouses function in relationship to each other. That is "what's important to know." Perhaps you will consider if it's possible to strengthen or mend your relationships—or reconnect—by changing what you expect of, and appreciate in, yourself and each other.

There is no doubt in my mind that those individuals who shared their stories in the preceding chapters hope that what they shared will make a positive difference in your life.

Finally, over the years of researching, writing and collaborating that went into this book, I became profoundly aware of the love and support of both my family of origin and the family my husband and I created.

I hope both hear my "thank you's" echoing down the sound waves of time.

Patricia Schudy
January 2017

Appendix I
Other Voices

Chapter 1. Different

In general when people think "daughter," they think protected or nurtured; but add "oldest" in front of it—it changes the definition. It makes the person a protector or nurturer. Oldest sons are raised to rule the world. Oldest daughters are raised to nurture it.

Jen, 31, oldest of three siblings

In some cultures, the oldest daughter is the first to be married and is given a special dowry. In our culture, being the oldest daughter means more responsibility, not more gifts showered upon you.

It's more of 'there's something required of you,' not something that would be given to you.

Kimi, 35, one younger brother

I always felt very alone because I didn't fit in. I wasn't one of the parents. I wasn't an adult. But I wasn't one of the kids. I don't think my sisters and brothers understand this.

"Leigh," 42 oldest of five siblings

I inherently knew I should be an example. I hated it. I always felt like an adult. I never got to have the fun. I was always aware. It was hard. My younger brothers and sister were more carefree. I don't think I had a childhood. I always felt like I had to walk the straight and narrow.

Gina," 50, oldest of four siblings

All the kids I ever knew who were 'cool' were the youngest in their families. The reasons were obvious. Their older siblings had taught them all the cool things.

"Mary Elizabeth," 45, oldest of four
in a blended family

When we were growing up, my brother would rattle my chain because he knew I'd get in trouble. It would make me angry, but my mother said, "Well, I don't care, you're the oldest, you should know better." My brother and I can both laugh about it now, but there was a time when we couldn't. Now I have a grandson and granddaughter and I watch them interact. I hear my granddaughter saying, "Nana, it wasn't my fault." I tell my daughter what it was like, but she can't envision that because she wasn't the oldest. She was the middle one. All I can do is let my granddaughter know I empathize with her.

Cindy, 61, one younger brother

Neither of my parents is an oldest child. I don't think they realize that they treated me differently and continue to treat me differently. It really doesn't bother me as an adult. As a child, however, I remember often feeling there was an injustice in the way I was treated and the way my sisters were treated. My sisters and parents used to say, "Who do you think you are, the Queen of Sheba?" But you know, the Queen of Sheba was a pretty smart chick. She knew how to take care of herself.

Jeanette, 35, oldest of three daughters

The difference in being an oldest daughter is that your focus is so much on other people whether it's dealing with parents or taking care of siblings—your sense of responsibility is different. You are challenged to be self-sufficient, especially if you have siblings and you're in a busy household, to help carry the load. I don't think there's anything wrong with being whatever position as long as you really feel like you are connected to your family as an individual. There's something in the oldest that likes to have control and thinks they know what's best. At the same time, there's a very contradicting expectation of being self-sacrificing. Other birth positions have different issues, but I don't think so many contradictions.

Wynne, 43, older of two daughters

I feel like everything I did in my life, I had to do it alone. I had to forge the path. My path might have been a little bit easier if would have had guidance and instruction from older siblings.

"Nancy," over 50, oldest of three siblings

Chapter 2. Born to Lead

My dad cut out on us when I was 14, and I had to get a job to help out my mom, so I became a leader and developed initiative.

Alison, 25, oldest of three siblings

My sister was the oldest child in our family. She graduated as an honor student with a double major in chemistry and biology. Seeing her walk across the stage in her black gown and hat with the red and gold tassels, I just thought she was awesome. It was amazing. She was definitely an inspiration in pursuing goals and letting no obstacles stop you. I would be a different person today if I had not had my oldest sister.

Margarita, 42, youngest of three siblings

Growing up, I was driven, insecure, talented, goal-oriented. Now I'm driven, intelligent, caring, compassionate, creative and self-aware—confident! As an oldest daughter, you realize there's a difference between being a leader and a manager. There are some pretty strong leadership qualities I acquired from being the oldest, and the expectations that were put on me. I don't think I would have been as successful as I have been without them.

Deb, 38, one younger sister

Chapter 3. Brought Up to Boss

My sister was bossy. She was the oldest, telling me what to do. Now she really is one of my best friends. I'd like it if she was just my friend instead of still acting like my big sister. I just like to have a lot of fun. She'd be more fun to be around if she didn't feel like she had to teach everybody a lesson all the time. That's also the experience I've had of older sisters of my friends. That they are bossier, whereas the younger sisters are more easygoing. It the nature of the beast of being the first-born girl.

"Electra," 26, middle child

I still function as the oldest daughter. When it comes to my mother's health, at least, much is deferred to me. Deference is the word I'd use, and it's a positive word."

Mary, 50, oldest of seven siblings

In my sister's defense (and in defense of all oldest daughters), I think there's this unspoken role or pressure that they feel to take care of everybody, to be the fixer of everything. But in my sister's efforts to control and keep everything in order, she can be a b——h sometimes."

"Lauren," 36, younger of two siblings

I would like to run everything. I'm already president of my own company. I step up to the plate and run things I'm not even supposed to be running.

"Kathryn," 60, older of two siblings

I definitely think I have a domineering trait. One of the nicknames for me among my friends is "master cylinder"—which means I'm going to have a point of view and drive it through. They mean that in a nice way, sort of. With business colleagues, I try to pull back. I try to make my opinion known, but I don't have to be the boss in professional situations. The younger me was much more judgmental—"My idea is good; your idea is bad." Professionally I've backed off a lot, but I still have confidence to interject when I think it's valid, to lead when I need to. I'm good at recognizing when a group needs a leader.

That translates to my family life now. With my siblings, I don't always have to be the leader now like I did when I was younger. With my husband, If I'm trying to make a decision on too big a thing, that's when I would hear about it—that I'm bossy. That's when I back off.

Suzanne, 45, oldest of four siblings

I admit to being bossy. When I was in pre school, the teacher told my mom I was better at directing kids how to play than at playing. It's something I remind myself of as an adult and try to get a handle on it. I've learned that to be loud does not mean that you are strong.

"Lynn," 34, one younger brother

I think sometimes when people are younger and feel the responsibility, they sometimes feel they need to be controlling and bossy even when they don't have to be. My sister changed when she no longer had the responsibility.

Annette, 52, third of ten siblings.

As adults, my sisters would let me know when I was going over the line, when I was being bossy. When I was traveling with them, I taught myself not to be the voice of authority. It's much more fun. I just kind of stepped back and allowed myself to be the helpee instead of the helper, and it was fabulous.

"Ronnie," 58, six younger siblings

I am a free-lance writer and author. I am my own boss and sometimes my boss is a b—-h!

Jeanette, 35, one younger sister

Chapter 4. Little Mothers

It's just different what an oldest sister does for younger sisters. To sum it up—they see me more as a mother, and I know them and their weaknesses, almost like their mother.

Leigh, 26, oldest of five daughters

I declared myself the mom of my brother when I was four years old! My mother said when my brother was being potty-trained, I took over. When I was ten, my dad was on the road every day. We didn't have much structure or rules, so I came to my mother and produced a list of daily chores for my brother and me. I became very mother-like when I was very young, but that led to some interesting struggles when I was a teenager.

"Lynn," 34, one brother *three years younger*

My sister had to do chores, take us places, do a lot things that mom probably could have done, but didn't. I think she was always trying to get my mother's approval.

Judy, 58, third of four siblings

When I came into childbearing age, I said I didn't want to have any children. That was as a result of the responsibilities I'd had. Later, when I realized I wanted children, it was too late.

Christina, 52, oldest of seven siblings

My sister's still the one we turn to for the mother-hen questions because she's responsible and caring, but she's not a taskmaster. She'd be the first to relinquish organizing if somebody else stepped up.

Rachel, 40, youngest of four siblings

I love my sisters, but I'd like them to stop wanting too much from me. I don't know who the real me is sometimes. I have a hard time doing things alone. I'm so used to taking care of people.

"Payton," 43, oldest of five daughters

Chapter 5. Response-ability

I was the one "old enough to know better"--always. It was my responsibility to stop whatever was wrong. That seemed unfair because I couldn't control the way anybody else acted, so why was it my fault? Most oldest daughters I've known seem tobe overly responsible and carry that trait as adults into being caretakers of the world.

Jan, 45, oldest of five siblings

I expected my oldest sister to be someone who would be there for me, meet my needs. I believed this was the way things work.

Julie 50, younger of two sisters

I always wanted to be an actress. Maybe if I hadn't felt so much responsibility in my early life, I would have had the free spirit to do that.

"Nancy," over 50, two younger siblings

Now that I'm an adult, I realize there are things I just don't need to do. I started saying "no" quite a few years ago when I feel I've taken on too much. There's been no reaction from family, but I still felt guilty. I'm getting used to it—it just takes a little bit of time. It's a matter of priorities.

"Jennifer," 37, one younger brother

My mother had a severe case of blood poisoning that lasted for months when my little sister was about four months old. I was three and a half. My mother said I became her hands. So from the time I was little, I was responsible. It made a big impact on me. Mother said people used to say I spoke like an old lady when I was a kid.

Joan, 62, one younger sister

I've had this role as the oldest daughter and have accepted it for a long time. It doesn't mean I like it, but I've accepted it. I believe I have choices. But because of my role that I've had all my life. I just never even think too much about all those other choices. Somebody has to hold the family together. It's not always fair. Sometimes you have to do what isn't fair or that you don't like. When we're older we have choices. However with regards to the family, it is our responsibility, not a choice, to make sure that our parents are happy, that our family stays together. It is left up to us to do those things. We really don't have a choice.

Ramona, 51, 3 younger brothers

Chapter 6. Siblingspeak

A lot of fun was being different from her. Specifically, "How can I be cooler than my sister?" I'd still like it if she was just my friend instead of still acting like my big sister. I'd like to tell her she'd be more fun to be around if she didn't feel like she had to teach everybody a lesson all the time.

"Electra," 26, middle child

Growing up, I took for granted that both my older sister and brother were there to meet my needs—and they were well met. As an older adult, I don't know if that's the way it 'should have been,' but it was a comfort to me.

As the younger daughter, I've always felt so protected. I don't think my sister felt that way. She felt a lot of responsibility. She felt she had to be the perfect daughter.

LaDonne, 72, third of four siblings

By the time the third girl—me—came along, it was 'okay, been there, done that.' There were certain talents that I'm only now aware of as an adult that I think would have been recognized and nurtured had I been first

"Jessie Buckminster," 49, third of four siblings

I know I'm not the only one out there who wants to read, "Surviving an Oldest Daughter." This has been a hard journey for me. I feel like I want to cry for a variety of reasons. I miss my sister with all my heart. I miss the fun times we had. I lost my best friend. I used to really resent her. I'm beyond that. I'm into acceptance. She cut herself off from my family and the life experience that you get from being involved. I kind of feel cheated. I'm really said and I miss what could have been.

Julie, 50, younger of two daughters

I've always felt like I've taken someone else's script and played it, but it really wasn't my role to play. My sister abdicated her position as oldest daughter, and I got it. My parents created the role in me by giving me a lot more responsibility than I should have had. I'm still pissed over the whole thing.

I would like to say to my older sister, "If I'd been the oldest daughter, I would have picked up the ball and run with it. It would have seemed more orderly, to do the responsible things and mentor the younger children. If you'd asked me to help you, to be a team, I wouldn't have these feelings I have today."

To parents, "Childhood is too valuable. You can't go back and reclaim it. Don't put your oldest daughter in a position where they're doing your job. No child should have that role. Being part of a family is sharing jobs. Helping is something all children should do.

To oldest daughters, "Try to be your own person. Your life is very valuable, and you can be a good daughter without sacrificing your life."

"Helen," 68, *middle of three daughters*

"I'd like to tell my sister to make her life just the way she wants it and not to be afraid to do that, not to be afraid to make whatever changes are necessary to feel good about herself, not to be afraid to fail. She's had a very hard life; she's earned it. She needs to have fun.

Pat, 52, eight years younger than only sibling

My sister, the oldest in our family, would intentionally use voice intimidation. She was a screamer, kind of a drama queen. My father was very threatening, had an intimidating voice. I think maybe she was just passing on what she had learned—the old "kick the cat" syndrome.

Craig, 44, youngest of three siblings

My older sister gets a little bit too much over the top when she gets into a deep passion about how she feels about something. She's intense at times. It could be that goes along with being the oldest daughter. At times I am intense too, but the difference is the way she reacts. She will at times forget to think about how it sounds.

"Marie," 44, third of five siblings

There were times I sat listening to her go on and on and on and thought, "Holy cow, how much longer is this going to last?" It was more info than I requested. It didn't give me the opportunity to think for myself. It was more telling me what to think.

Jane, 37, youngest of three daughters

My oldest sister's off-the cuff comments like, "Your hair looks stupid," or "Why are you wearing that?' made me self-conscious.

"Sarah," 47, third of six siblings.

Chapter 7. Ties that Bind

A friend told me in her country it's very common for an oldest child to marry the youngest child of another family. I think the explanation is that the oldest child tends to nurture the youngest child; the youngest depends on the oldest, and so that balances out.

Mary 21, oldest of six siblings

I grew up raising my brothers and I think that experience shaped who I am now. My husband has a sister who's three years older and a ten-years-younger brother. In our marriage, I'm the "take-charge" person. My husband doesn't make the decisions. It's a bone of contention for us. I totally want him to. He just doesn't care. He's like, "whatever..."

Julia, 26, *wo younger brothers*

It's tough being married to an oldest daughter. I think once an oldest daughter is married, she should be a wife. But that's not the way it works. My wife wants to be the boss. It's always a power struggle. That's the way the oldest-daughter syndrome works. She figures the way something should be and does it that way. I'm a byproduct of what she wants to do. She thinks it's her obligation to see that everything's working right. That takes time away from me and our relationship, but I resent the conflict more than the time.

"Parker," 68, oldest son married to oldest daughter

My wife is the oldest child in her family. She has one brother, who's a year younger. We've been married seven years and have one daughter who's three. Her family has never relied on her regarding more responsibilities. She always keeps her composure, is humble, kind, courteous, caring, well read, independent and pragmatic. Some of these characteristics are probably a result of being the oldest daughter and the oldest child. She was the first out of her house, the first to have a career, the first to get married, the first to have a child. In my opinion, she did all those things very well. I think I am fortunate.

"Earnest," 35, younger of two sons

My husband's the youngest son. He gets frustrated with me because it's hard for me to relate to being the youngest and to being reluctant to speak up to the older ones. Even at age forty-one, he's still the youngest brother. He'll always be junior in terms of asking for what he wants and giving his opinion. I'd like to ask him to act like the oldest for a while, but I don't think he'd ask me to change how I am.

Robyn, 40, oldest of three daughters

I would love it if my husband would take care of me, but it's too much to ask. I have this intuition about other people's needs. He doesn't have this.

Helen, 44, only daughter, middle child

I've been divorced three times. It took me forever to realize that I was absolutely looking for someone who would look after me.

Ann, 48, oldest of eight siblings

I'm married to an oldest. I think the oldest-oldest combination is both good and bad. The oldest is very responsible, and it's harder for oldests to relax and enjoy things. We both value being responsible, I'm happy that we expect that from each other. There's a comfort in that. It would be frustrating if the person we were married to wasn't responsible. But as you get older, you realize a need for balance. Responsibility can be a strain. It takes a toll on anybody.

Robin, 53, oldest of 3 daughters

It would be a great relief in a relationship to not always be the one to be the first to step up to assume a burden.

"Anna," 54, one younger brother

I don't know that it's important to know the birth-order position in choosing a mate. I think what's more important is what you both are expecting, want in a relationship and are willing to give to the relationship.

"Clarissa," 54, oldest of six siblings

My husband is a middle child. I've never thought about his birth order. We've been married thirty years. Over the years I've heard him say that one of the things he's happy about in our relationship is that I take care of myself, do what I need to do, and am not a dependent person. I don't think there's anything wrong with wanting to be taken care of, but I'm much more at ease being the caregiver.

"Roxanne," 59, oldest of four siblings

I'd like to be more "taken care of" by my husband.

Claudia, 56, two younger siblings

If there is any advantage to my being married to an oldest daughter, it would be that she was able to spend a great deal of time observing the value system of her parents. It gave her a sense of responsibility and also allegiance and commitment to her parents' well-being. She realized early on that any type of later-year caregiving was going to fall on her shoulders.

She has very, very high standards with respect to how she lives and performs her day-to-day tasks and activities. She tends to expect the same level of performance from others. I'd certainly think anyone considering marrying an oldest daughter would have an advantage knowing that the person he's about to marry is a perfectionist, for example, and that he might be held to the same standards.

Bill, 67, middle of three siblings

Chapter 8. Across Borders

The entire chapter is comprised of Other Voices.

Chapter 9. Change, Please

There's an enormous gap between me and my siblings. I felt the pressure to get out in a way they never did. They don't realize that their childhood was different than mine. I was often asked to make sacrifices: "This is important for your sisters. You are just going to have to understand." For them, there's this collective sense of parents who went the extra mile for them; but from my point of view, I was one who also made sacrifices for them.

I never asked to be the oldest of five children. Getting out has made all the difference in my life. Now there's nobody holding me back, nobody telling me what to do. I feel like I make my own destiny.

"Leigh" 42, oldest of five siblings

"I'd like to not be so stressed. I'd like to be more laid back.

Alison, 25, oldest of three siblings

I want oldest daughters to know they have choices, that they're not obligated by expectations, that when they are adults they have choices. That's what changed my life.

"Lynn," 34, one younger brother

Chapter 10. Selfies

If we learn how to temper our perfectionism. If we stop being too demanding. If we change our "people can't do it right, so we have to do it" attitude. That's our biggest problem. If we do these things, we can create a lot of powerful people around us. If we step back, in our families, in our jobs, others will step up and they will bring a lot to the table.

"Ruth," 57, one older brother, four younger siblings

If I had a daughter, I would be very careful with what kind of responsibilities I gave her.

Julia, 26, oldest of five siblings

We have a history of not telling each other what's going on in our individual lives. I wish we truly knew one another. How wonderful it would be if we could sit down once again as a family—siblings—and have a discussion, looking into our hearts for what the real truth is.

"Grace," 72, oldest child, four younger brothers

I couldn't have moved away from both my parents and found out who I am without a person like my mom in my life. Being the oldest and being raised by her, a youngest child, created a balance. Even though I couldn't always relate to it, that's made me able today to express love and happiness, to kick off my shoes and play.

"Lynn" 34, one younger brother

If I could give advice to parents of an oldest daughter, I would say, "Be encouraging, positive. Somehow let her know that it's okay to be different, to stand out, to search or go in a different direction. Tell her to be true to herself. Tell her it's okay to make a mistake."

"Gina," 50, oldest of four siblings

Of course oldest daughters can be carefree, but they choose not to be. Instead, they choose to take the safe route—don't rock the boat, don't make anybody mad, do what's expected.

I never had control in my life until I was fifty-one years old. Now I'm sixty. It's a brand new age. Now there will be no one else in control of my life. I'm in charge. I'm not completely done with me yet. So even though I really don't care anymore what people think of me, I'm not a spontaneous person in some respects. But I'm getting better.

Joyce, 60, one younger sister

Oldest daughters can step out of expectations and find who they really are and also to become more carefree. Most would need help. It's tough.

I get overwhelmed quite often because of the expectations I place on myself, probably a result of my experiences growing up. I'm trying to let go of things I'm not in control of. I'm trying to prioritize, to have my husband and my children come first.

As an adult, I know I have the right to develop non-oldest daughter characteristics. I don't know if it will happen, but I have the right to do it. I'd like to think it's possible for me.

Stephanie, 35, one younger sister

I love my family deeply. We are extremely tight, well-knit. I still function as the oldest daughter. I think the sooner you realize that it truly is your life and you don't have to feel like you're so enmeshed with all the other stuff, the easier it is to be the oldest daughter.

Mary, 50, oldest of six siblings

I would like a closer relationship with my sister. I'm not sure what it would take. It's almost as if we're from two different planets. We do not have the same values.

Clarissa," 54, five younger siblings

I'd like to be more free like my younger brother. He does whatever he wants. I would love to have that freedom. If I'd really done what my heart wanted me to do, I'd have pursued the arts. One day maybe I'll do that.

Kelly, 35, oldest of three siblings

I wonder if there's a desire in oldest daughters to get credit for what they do and have done.

Cathy, 51, one younger sister

My biggest expectation today is that we'll get along. I think it's more important to me than it is to them. Sometimes I'd like to experience being more "taken care of." I'd like an acknowledgment of all of the taking care of that I've done.

Beth, 36, two younger sisters

I strive for excellence, but now it's for me and my future family. I expect to be very successful. I meet my own expectations. (Chuckle). I'm often surprised that I can do what I do!

April, 34, oldest of three siblings

I think women who are oldest daughters can help oldest daughters growing up—just by letting them know that someone understands what they're going through and why they're going through it.

Claudia, 56, oldest of three siblings

Twice in the last year I've been able to ask my brother in an authentic way for his advice on an issue I was struggling with. They were some of the most connected conversations with him I've ever had—deep and important and serious.

Michelle, 40, one younger brother

I LOVED being the oldest. When people ask if I have brothers and sisters, I say, "Yes, and I'm the oldest and don't forget it!"

Suzanne, 45, oldest of four siblings

Appendix II
Survey Snapshots

The questions and answers cited below are taken from the author's online surveys. They were selected for their relevance to each chapter. The highest number of responses to any given question is shown. These percentages may be low if respondents were given a lengthy list of choices. In those cases, when answers most often selected are separated by one or two percent, both are reported. The percentages are shown with numbers and the percent sign (e.g., 25%) for easier reading.

Note: The following information is not intended to be read or interpreted as statistically valid. The answers are "snapshots" of the survey participants' opinions. The percentages are based on the varying number of respondents in each category.

Chapter 1. Different

From survey section for oldest daughters:

Q. *At what age did you first realize that things were expected of you that were not expected of your sisters and/or brothers?*

A. Before age eight, 41%; Between the ages of eight and fifteen years old, 56%

Q. How would your life be different today if you had not been the oldest daughter?

A. Not so self-critical, 31%

Q. *Did you have more or fewer responsibilities growing up than your siblings?*

A. More, 9%; Fewer, 51%; No difference, 30%

From survey section for siblings:

Q. *Did the oldest daughter in your family have more responsibilities, expectations, or higher standards growing up than her siblings?*

A. More, 30%; Fewer, 33%; No difference, 36%.

Chapter 2. Born to Lead

From survey section for oldest daughters:

Q. *Were there more responsibilities, expectations, or higher standards for you growing up than for your brother(s) and/or sister(s)?*

A. Yes, 89%

Q. *Does your occupation today involve a significant amount of caregiving, leadership, neither or both?*

A. Leadership 31%; Caregiving, 18%; Both, 32%; Neither, 18%.

Chapter 3. Brought Up to Boss

From survey section for oldest daughters:

Q. *Were you responsible for the behavior of your siblings when they were children, teenagers, neither or both?*

A. When siblings were children, 35%; When siblings were teens, 2%; Neither, 41%; Both, 22%.

From survey section for siblings:

Q. *Was the oldest daughter in your family responsible for the behavior of you and/or your siblings when you were children, teenagers, neither or both?*

A. When children, 30%; When teens, 2%; Neither, 59%; Both, 9%

Chapter 4. Little Mothers

The survey did not ask if oldest daughters were ever responsible for the *care* of their siblings. It only surveyed responsibility for *behavior* as reported in Chapter 3.

Q. *What word (from a wide-ranging list) do you most associate with the oldest daughter in your family?*

A. No word garnered a majority. The word most often selected was "caring," 16%

Chapter 5. Response-ability

This question drew almost totally opposite responses from oldest daughters and siblings.

From survey section for oldest daughters:

Q. *Are there the same "oldest daughter" expectations of you as an adult that there were when you were growing up?*

A. Yes, 65%; No, 34%

From survey section for siblings:

Q. *Are there the same expectations of the oldest daughter in your family now that she's an adult as there were when you were all growing up?*

A. Yes, 26%; No, 74%

Chapter 6. Siblingspeak

Q. *What doesn't an oldest daughter "get" about how her siblings feel about her?*

A. She's admired and respected, 27%; No one expects her to be perfect, 26%; She needs to listen more; her opinion is not always wanted, 25%

Q. If you could give her any advice, what would it be?

A. Let go of resentment, 15%; Take better care of herself, 14%.

Q. What words you least *associate with the oldest daughter in your family?*

A. Carefree, 22%; Easy-going, 21%

Chapter 7. Ties that Bind

From survey section for spouses:

Q. *Whose life would be most changed if your wife stopped filling expectations as an oldest daughter?*

A. Hers, 39%; Her parents', 17%; Her siblings', 17%; Our new family's, 6%; Mine, 6%

Chapter 8. Across Borders

From survey section for oldest daughters:

Q. Which of the following words would you most associate with yourself?

A. African American responders: Responsible
Asian American responders: Responsible
Hispanic/Latino responders: Responsible
Middle Eastern responders: Responsible, Critical of Self, Strong
Combined from all responders, including above: Responsible

Q. Which of the following words would you associate least with yourself?

A. African American: Self-centered
Asian American: Carefree
Hispanic/Latino: Privileged
Middle Eastern: Self-centered
All: including other ethnicities: Carefree

Q. *Were there more responsibilities, expectations or higher standards for you growing up than for your brothers/sisters?*

A. African American: Yes, 92%; No, 8%
Asian American: Yes, 90%; No, 10%

Hispanic/Latino: Yes, 85%; No, 15%
Middle Eastern: Yes, 100%
All, including other ethnicities: Yes, 90%; No, 10%

Q. *At what age did you first realize that things were expected of you that weren't expected of your sisters/brothers:*

A. African American: Before age eight, 49%; Between eight and fifteen, 51%
Asian American: Before age eight, 58%; Between eight and fifteen, 37%
Hispanic/Latino: Before age eight, 29%; Between eight and fifteen, 64%
Middle Eastern: Before age eight, 25%; Between eight and fifteen, 50%
All of the above plus other ethnicities:
Before age eight, 42%; Between eight and fifteen, 56%

Q. *Are there the same "oldest daughter" expectations of you as an adult as there were when you were growing up?*

A. African American: Yes, 79%; No, 21%
Asian American: Yes, 75%; No, 25%
Hispanic/Latino: Yes, 80%; No, 20%
Middle Eastern: Yes, 50%; No, 50%
All, including other ethnicities:
Yes, 65%; No, 35%

Chapter 9. Change, Please

From survey section for oldest daughters:

Q. What words would you least associate with yourself?

A. Carefree, 20%

From survey section for siblings:

The answer to the same question, as also noted in Chapter 6: Carefree, 22%; Easy-going, 21%

Another question on both the oldest-daughter and the sibling sections of the survey perhaps sheds more light on the above question and answers.

Q. What's the biggest disadvantage of being the oldest daughter?

A. Oldest daughters: The pressure to be perfect; A. Siblings: The pressure to be perfect.

Chapter 10. Selfies

Q. *If you could have chosen your birth-order position, what would you choose?*

A. Oldest, 60%; Middle, 15%; Youngest, 23%

Endnotes

Chapter 2. Born to Lead

Partial list of oldest daughters who are currently leaders, or were during their lifetime, in their field of endeavor. Alphabetical by last name:

- **Madeline Albright**, first woman U.S. Secretary of State
- **Gwendolyn Brooks**, poet and author, and the first African-American to receive the Pulitzer Prize for Poetry
- **Julia Child**, chef and author, introduced French cuisine to American audiences
- **Shirley Chisholm**, first African American woman elected to U.S. Congress
- **Sandra Cisneros**, award-winning American writer
- **Hillary Clinton,** U.S. Secretary of State and the first woman nominee of major political party for U.S.
- **Wangari Maathai**, first woman in East/Central Africa to earn doctorate degree, the 2004 Nobel Laureate for peace
- **Idina Menzel,** award-winning actress and singer known for her role as Elphaba in the Broadway show *Wicked* and as the voice of Elsa in the movie *Frozen*
- **Angela Merkel,** chancellor of Germany, recognized as world leader

- **Kate Middleton**/Catherine, Duchess of Cambridge, member of British Royal Family who speaks out on behalf of children
- **Mary Tyler Moore**, Emmy-award winning actor
- **Sandra Day O'Connor**, first woman appointed to U.S. Supreme Court
- **Rosa Parks**, American civil rights activist
- **Frances Perkins**, U.S. Secretary of Labor, first woman appointed to the U.S. Cabinet
- **Sally Ride**, astronaut, first American woman in space
- **Linda Rodriguez**, poet and award-winning mystery writer
- **J.K. Rowling**, author of the best-selling *Harry Potter* series
- **Eleanor Roosevelt**, U.S. First Lady as wife of President Franklin D. Roosevelt, activist and diplomat
- **Aung San Suu Kyii**, state counselor of Myanmar, 1991 Nobel Laureate for Peace
- **Sheryl Sandberg**, COO of Facebook
- **Sonia Sotomayor**, first person of Hispanic heritage to serve on the U.S. Supreme Court
- **Meryl Streep**, Academy Award winning actress
- **Pat Summitt**, former head basketball coach of University of Tennessee Lady Volunteers, retired in 2012 with NCAA record 1,028 victories; acclaimed for

leadership in sharing publicly her diagnosis of Alzheimer's

- **Maria Tallchief**, the first Native American major prima ballerina
- **Venus Williams**, the first African-American—male or female—to rank No. 1 in the world of tennis

Resources

Non-fiction Books by Oldest Daughters
Alphabetical by author's last name:

Madam Secretary: A Memoir, **Madeleine Albright**

The French Chef Cookbook, **Julia Child**

Unbought *and Unbossed*, **Shirley Chisholm**

A House of My own: Stories of My Life, **Sandra Cisneros**

Unbowed: A Memoir, **Wangari Maathai**

The Majesty of the Law: Reflections of a Supreme Court Justice, **Sandra Day O'Connor**

To Space and Back, **Sally Ride** and and Susan Obie

The Autobiography of Eleanor Roosevelt, **Eleanor Roosevelt**

Lean In: Women, Work and the Will to Lead, **Sheryl Sandberg**

And one more thing before you go, **Maria Shriver**

My Beloved World, **Sonia Sotomayor**. Spanish edition: *Mi Mundo Adorado*

Reach for the Summit, **Pat Summitt**

Maria Tallchief: America's Prima Ballerina, **Maria Tallchief** and Larry Kaplan

I am Malala: The Girl Who Stood Up for Education and Who Was Shot by the Taliban, **Malala Yousafzai** and Christina Long. Spanish edition: *Yo Soy Malala*

Fictional works about Oldest Daughters

America's First Daughter, Stephanie Dray and Laura Kamoie.

Frozen, Junior novel by Disney Book Group

Websites

banbossy.com
bowentheoryacademy.org
enneagram.net
firstladieslibrary.org/biographies
www.supremecourt.gov/about/biographies.aspx

Publications

Kluger, Jeffrey. *The Science of Siblings*. Time, Inc. Specials, 201

Permissions

Kira Salak, *The White Mary*
Leigh Standley, *Curly Girl Design*
Abraham Verghese, *Cutting for Stone*

Acknowledgments

This book, about family relationships, could not have been written and published without the assistance of several "families."

My Personal Family. My husband Robin and our five adult children contributed their individual professional skills toward the book's completion. Eric recommended the hosting platform for my first oldest-daughter website and identified survey instruments for me to use. Kristin gave her psychologist's feedback on wording for the survey, wrote the book's foreword and created the "Professional Insight" and "For Reflection" sections. Annie took it upon herself to monitor me, to let me know when I needed to step back from intense writing schedules, take a break, enjoy holidays. Scott collaborated on the establishment and naming of our publishing company and regularly urged me to keep writing and going toward my goal despite any obstacles. Brian, as described below, contributed his unique line-editing skills. They loved me through the sometimes seemingly endless steps along the way to the book's completion.

My Family of origin. My parents Charles and Matilda Hellinger started all this, taught, guided and loved me. My (all younger) siblings Carole Barnickel, Sharon Townsend-Kovak, Charles Hellinger, Jr., and Dr. Deborah Hellinger allowed me to explore their memories and feelings and trusted that I would represent our family fairly and accurately. Our friendships have only grown over the years. Carole has also for years provided critical "first-reader" feedback on my writing, including pages in this book.

My Writing Family. The Writer's Group in Kansas City met regularly for several years. Author Barbara Bartocci believed in this book's concept from the beginning, provided non-stop cheerleading and encouragement, read every iteration and provided unpaid editing services. Free-lance writer Nora Ellen Richard and novelist D'Ann Dreiling listened critically to drafts and rewrites for six years and encouraged me to keep writing because of what they said they learned for and about their own families. The four of us happen to be oldest or only daughters. Then we were joined by Karla Autrey, a skilled storyteller who contributed her younger-sibling perspective and who says that now she, too, can almost always spot an oldest daughter.

My Editing Family. Developmental editor Sony Hocklander, an experienced newspaper writer and editor in both print and electronic media. She analyzed the structure of the book to ensure that it flowed easily and logically from the first chapter to the last. She read my manuscript thoroughly, made every effort to understand what I hoped to bring to the reader, and was spot-on in her editing and revising suggestions. Sony is a true professional. I am fortunate to have worked with her.

Line editor Brian Schudy meticulously combed the pages of my drafts, monitoring the length and pacing of each sentence and paragraph. He caught what could have slowed down or stopped the reader. His job was made either easier or harder because he is my son. I leave it to him to say which, but I am grateful that he courageously took me on as a client.

Formatting editor Mike Lance. He worked to ensure the book's interior reflected professionalism and consistency and then uploaded the book in the required formats to publishers. My gratitude also to poet and oldest daughter Maril Crabtree for suggesting Mike. Without his services, I might still be spending time struggling to figure out how to do technical things that are not in my area of expertise.

Cover Artist and Book Designer Ann-Marie Greenberg. She listened to my various ideas for a cover and translated them into visuals—which after a while convinced me I should allow her to be the artist she is at her core. Set free from my pre-conceived ideas, she used her imagination and talents to create the book's cover design that I am so proud of.

In addition to my personal, writing and editing families are individuals to whom I also express much appreciation.

Individual practitioners of the Bowen Family Systems Theory. (The late) Donald J. Shoulberg, Ph.D.; Margaret Otto, LSCSW; Dori Moore, LSCSW; Carroll Hoskins, LSCSW; and Michael E. Kerr, M.D., Emeritus Director of the Bowen Center for the Study of the Family. They shared their professional expertise when I began my exploration of the role of oldest daughters within families.

Lanti Riederer and Noreen Purcell, oldest daughters and trusted friends, provided honest, informal feedback about issues in various chapters. Mary Jo Biersmith became a valuable go-to person when I needed an outsider's "insider" opinion about the authenticity of sibling experiences or sentiments in various chapters. A high-school and college classmate who passed away before the book was completed, she was the younger daughter in a family of four siblings.

Members of the "Brainstorming" writer's group in Colorado, especially authors Lura Fischer, Linda Kinnamon, Amanda Mageras, and Don Calloway. They generously shared their publishing experiences.

Finally, thank you to the hundreds of individuals who provided the survey responses and personal stories that are the core of this book. And to the hundreds more who participated in the survey whose stories or responses do not appear but who helped me recognize which issues were important to include. I am especially grateful to these individuals who knew me only through the survey, my website, or the telephone and who trusted me with their experiences and feelings. Without you, this book would not exist.

About the author, psychologist, and cover artist

Patricia Schudy is a former nationally syndicated youth columnist. After more than three decades of also writing bylined features as Pat Schudy for regional and national newspapers and magazines, she spent several years in organizational leadership on behalf of youth. She continues to enjoy oldest-daughter conversations through her website and blog at oldestdaughter.com. This native Midwesterner now resides in Colorado.

Kristin Schudy Russell is a clinical psychologist who has specialized in women's issues and postpartum depression for the past ten years. She enjoys teaching women the importance of caring for themselves with the same grace and love they offer to others. www.kristinrussellphd.com Dr. Russell resides in Colorado with her husband and their three sons.

Ann Marie Greenberg is a middle daughter and an artist living in Chicago, Illinois. She teaches art to young children and creates paintings, prints and sculptures. You can find her work at https://amgreenbergartwork.tumblr.com

About the cover

The illustration is intended to express the joy and the burdens of being an oldest daughter. She is willingly tethered to her family and forging her own path. We can learn from her as she goes on her journey. (Artist's description)

Printed in Great Britain
by Amazon

25723306R00138